"Excellent! Exciting! Extraordinary! John Powers captures the ageless Spirit of Truth that addresses our day. He travels back in time to 'interview' seven mystics who share their wisdom with candor, warmth, and good humor. Don't be fooled by Powers's deceptively simple style. He effectively channels the energy of every one of these spiritual giants. Repeatedly, we catch a glimpse of Divine Mystery. We hear the Word that our age urgently needs to hear."

The Catholic Sun

"*Holy & Human* is excellent. I welcome this fine volume as a splendid addition to books on mysticism. It makes the mystical life approachable for all who seek it."

Sr. Ritamary Bradley
St. Ambrose University

"John Powers, a Passionist priest, offers here his imaginative conversations 'with seven of the most hope-filled incarnational mystics of the Western, Christian tradition.' He hopes by these interviews to place 'ordinary men and women, extraordinarily alive to the 'Aliveness of God,' in the context of their lives."

Theology Digest

"If you are just beginning to read some of the church's mystical literature, this charming book by Father Powers is a nice prelude to deeper studies. Most of us know Teresa of Avila, and Julian of Norwich has enjoyed a recent revival; but some of these mystics of centuries past are relatively unknown—forgotten saints whose writings are just being rediscovered. Father Powers brings their thought quite effectively into our own, very different, times. Who are Hildegard, Mechtild, and Jan Van Ruysbroeck? They are real people, both wholly and holy human."

Alice Lippeatt
Catholic Standard

"How about a book with 'interviews' conducted with Meister Eckhart, Hildegard of Bingen, and other medieval mystics? I thought the idea was pretty wild and I didn't think John Powers would be able to pull it off. But he did. As a device to show how 'humanness and holiness are intertwined,' it is effective."

Spirituality Today

"Powers's book is a feat of efficiency. Not only does it bring several medieval personalities to life, it gives them a chance to speak to today's issues and thus suggests deeper responses to modern conundrums."

Canadian Catholic Review

"The novelty of this approach helps make the thought and method of these mystics more open and appealing to our times. Father Powers gives us an exciting commentary on what they actually wrote."

The Priest

"In *Holy & Human,* John Powers provides a gallery of 'holy human men and women of yesterday who have shown us how to climb the mountain of God, with eyes that see in the dark.' His successful 'interviews' with seven mystics make them appear as the eminent guides they are, who speak to our own times."

Prairie Messenger

"John D. Powers reaches back to the Middle Ages to 'interview' seven 'gifted visionaries whose spiritual insights and wisdom have much to say to our fractured...age.'"

One World

JOHN D. POWERS

HOLY & HUMAN

MYSTICS FOR OUR TIME

Conversations with

HILDEGARD OF BINGEN
MECHTILD OF MAGDEBURG
MEISTER ECKHART
JAN VAN RUYSBROECK
JOHANNES TAULER
JULIAN OF NORWICH
TERESA OF AVILA

TWENTY-THIRD PUBLICATIONS
Mystic, Connecticut 06355

In memory of a master mensch:
Aquinas McGurk C.P.
Thanks

Third printing 1996

Twenty-Third Publications
185 Willow Street
P.O. Box 180
Mystic, CT 06355
(203) 536-2611
800-321-0411

ISBN 0-89622-398-1
Library of Congress Catalog Number 89-50565

Acknowledgments

My writing does not express what I know as much as it reveals what I am learning and becoming. I recognize very clearly that what I have learned and have become are due to the loving influence of cherished friends. So often each day I thank God for the people, living and deceased, who have shared their souls with me and who have helped me to look deeply into my own. This book is one way of giving life in the measure I have abundantly received it from friends, community, and family.

Like so many authors, I have learned over the years that although the art of writing may seem to be a rather egotistical endeavor, it is a creative process that demands a true self-forgetfulness, a death of sorts. In light of this letting-go so that something life-giving might be born, let me say thank you to all who have encouraged my imagination, daring, and patience. Without offering individual accolades for specific contributions, I list the names of those who have helped me and this book become.

Rick Frechette C.P., Fr. Fran Roberge, Mark Dupont, Matthew Leavy, O.S.B., Mary Alvine Maynard, Mary Bennett, Bill Murphy C.P., Tom Pollard, Fr. Leo Leclerc, Brian Beneat, Terence Kristofak C.P., Joe Sedley C.P., Joseph Saldanha S.J., Leo and Gerrie Frechette, Roger Elliott C.P. and the Passionist Community, the Parishioners of St. Rose de Lima Parish in Chicopee, Massachusetts, the Retreatants of Holy Family Retreat in West Hartford, Connecticut, and the Community of St. Anselm Abbey in Manchester, New Hampshire.

I thank also the inspiring men and women of Twenty-Third Publications who constantly encourage me to write. I especially appreciate the creative work of two talented editors at Twenty-Third Publications: Stephen Scharper and Patricia Kluepfel.

Contents

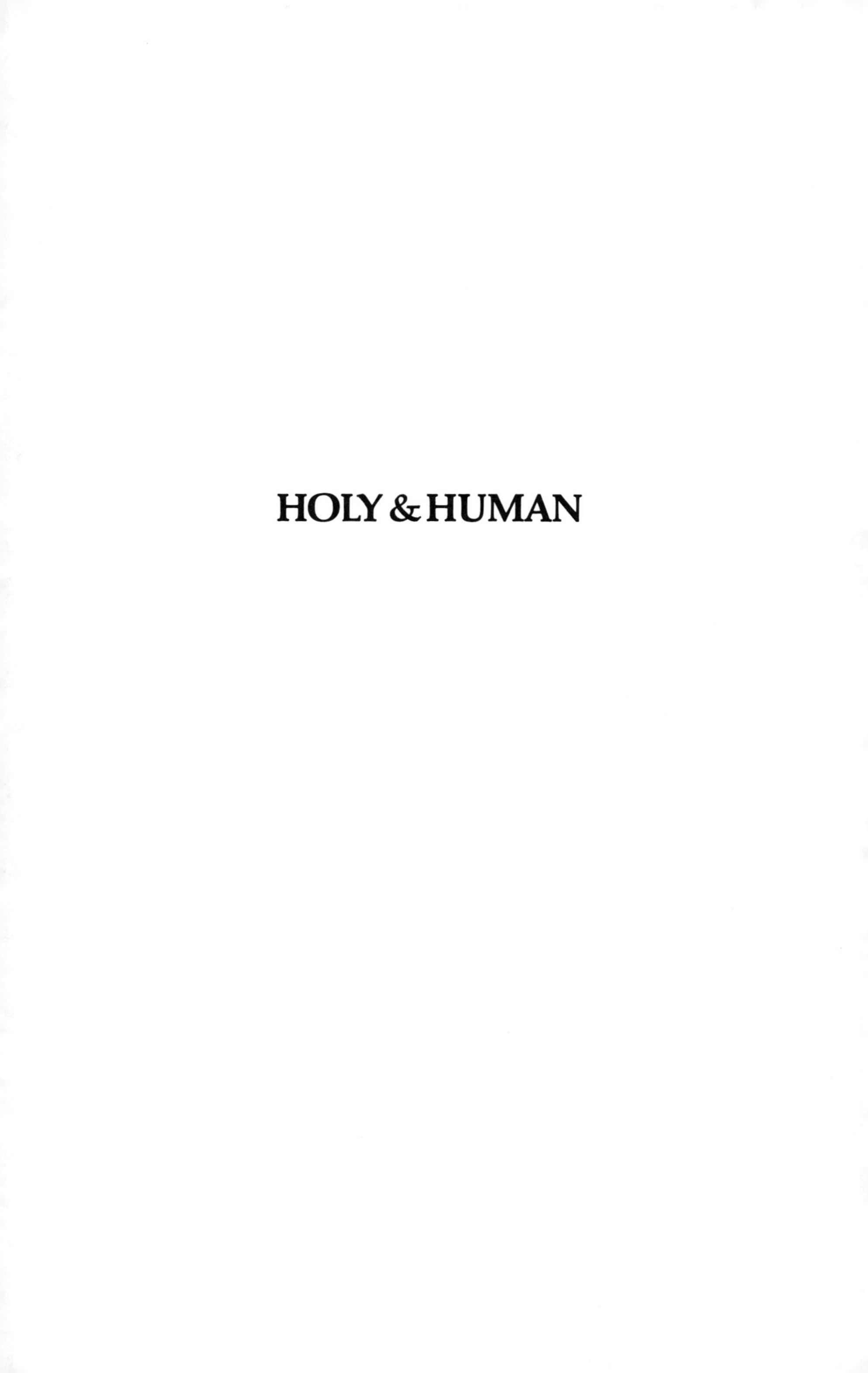

HOLY & HUMAN

Introductory Letter

Dear Reader,

Rather than writing a formally structured introduction to these imaginative interviews with seven of the most hope-filled incarnational mystics of the Western, Christian tradition, I have chosen to address a letter directly to you, with the hope that reading this book will be as fulfilling an adventure for you as the research and writing were for me.

Before I describe in detail where we shall travel in this book, let me welcome you to the journey to the past we shall take together, all for the purpose of living holier human lives in the future.

As one God-seeker to another, I know the demanding effort and healthy foolishness required simply to pick up a book with the word "mystic" in the title. For far too many, just the word "mystic" would conjure up negative images and threatening expectations. Let me assure you, then, at the start, that this book is meant to encourage your faith in yourself and others, widen your vision of the God who is Aliveness in the world, and build up hope where fear may have ruled. It is to remind you that the goal of Christian living is not to become other-worldly eccentrics, flawlessly perfect oddballs, obsessive "ferverts" (those who pervert healthy zeal and fervor), or even shadowy strangers who lurk on the fringes of human society and interaction. The ultimate goal of Christian living and, therefore, positive spirituality and mysticism is to help you live as these mystics lived: perfectly imperfect, holy, healthy, and hope-filled human lives.

The fundamental perspective that humanness and holiness are so intertwined that you cannot have one without the other was seared into my mind and soul by the master teacher to whose memory this book is dedicated. In my imagination, I can still see Aquinas McGurk saying as clearly as he did in class so many years ago, "If you want to be holy, and if you want to be a good priest (mother, father, friend, sister, brother, neighbor, Christian, Jew, or Hindu), strive first to be a good and healthy human being." What this influential guide did for me, I hope your meetings with the seven mystics interviewed in this book will do for you: tear holiness out of its prison of specialness, free the experience of God from the exclusive halls of cloistered rarity, while challenging the belief that mystics are a different species of human and somehow better. I hope the three male and four female mystics in this book will confirm what is already in your heart: the knowledge that in ordinary life God can be seen, touched, heard, and tasted with the senses of the heart, that God is revealed every day through the struggles of poverty, made manifest in the conflicting course of human emotion, disclosed in every relationship, and betrayed in the suffering of all people. God is uttered amid solitude, silence, and loneliness, confessed through sin and despair, expressed through the imagination, made public in and through history and the social environment. God cries out from the earth we take so much for granted, and is proclaimed with zeal and vulnerability through the Scriptures, sacraments, and gathered people of God.

Whether you are man or woman, barkeep or nun, nurse or monk, father, mother, teen student, baker, priest, construction worker, or lawyer, you too are called to become a mystic in your everyday living. To reinforce this point, I have chosen to interview seven individual men and women of the past who have profoundly opened my heart, mind, soul, and body to the sacredness of the created universe and the holiness of our shared humanness.

The interviewees, who taught me and can teach you how to live more spiritually and emotionally fulfilling lives in the future, were chosen precisely because they have been labeled "mystics" in the flow of history. Yet they were people very uncomfortable with any label that might set them apart from or above the ordinary human path toward God. Rather than seeing themselves as uniquely gifted with more of God than others might have, these men and women were often dragged screaming through the illusions of life, finding greater sanity, serenity, and sanctity in the acceptance of God.

They were ordinary men and women, extraordinarily alive to the Aliveness of God. They were God-seekers seduced to humanness by the affirming grace of God, God-seers wide-eyed to the color of divinity in every human interaction, spiritual sensitives filled with the wondrous intuition that every coincidence seeps with the eternal mystery of God, and sages of the imagination which ever flows with the rushing river of God's Is-ness. This is what you and I are called to become.

By imaginatively traveling back in time to interview them in the context of their lives I hope that you may not only be opened to the movements of God in the context of your life but that you might also be touched by their spirit of hope in the face of despairing odds, struck awake by their intense curiosity in an age of sleepy ignorance, and challenged by their compassion in a time of terror. I especially hope that as you meet each of them you will receive what I have received, a deep confidence that God can be and most often is found in the holy ground of creation and the holy stuff of humanity. With such a discovery, I hope your individual life, with its successes and failures, pains and joys, as well as the life of the church, with its tendency toward over-institutionalization as well as its zealous desire to be of service to God in the world, will be ignited with a very small spark of God's hope, God's daring, God's youthfulness, and God's confidence in the potential of all that is creatively evolving.

There have been many books and articles written that attempt to analyze the mystic phenomena. This will not be one of them. Rather than dissect the experience of God as though it were a matter of mere logic and rationality, I have chosen to relate actively to seven historical figures by sitting down (in my imagination) and interviewing them. Through this method, I hope to discover who they are as people in search of God, so that you may grow to like or dislike them, to learn from them, or be challenged by them.

Before introducing the mystics I have interviewed, I would like to share a general description of what a mystic is. I am confident that as a struggling Christian believer like myself, you would assent to the fundamental statements of Mary Wolf-Salin when she lists the basic beliefs of the Christian: "1) There is within us something beyond our understanding and control which has a certain power over our consciousness and lives, with which we must connect in order to live in a healthy way, 2) that this 'something' cannot be adequately understood without the note of 'divinity' being included, and 3) that this something is able to relate to us as subject to object."[1] The mystic in us all, that original spark of God, that soul-identity that is waiting to come out clearly, would not only agree with Wolf-Salin but would assent with body, mind, and soul in such a way that his or her life would be continually transformed into an image of the "something divine."

A believing Christian becomes a mystic when his or her life is so open, exposed, and vulnerable to the "divine something" and "someone" that he or she becomes what Rabbi Harold Kushner in *When All You've Wanted Isn't Enough* describes as a "mensch," a person of integrity:

> To be a mensch is to be the kind of person God had in mind when he arranged for human beings to evolve, someone who is honest, reliable, wise enough to be no longer naive but not yet cynical, a person you can trust to give you advice for your benefit rather than his or her own. A mensch acts not out of fear or out of desire to make a good impression but out of a strong inner conviction of who he or she is and what he or she stands for. A mensch is not a saint or a perfect person but a person

from whom all falsehood, all selfishness, and all vindictiveness have been burned away so that only a pure self remains. A mensch is whole and is one with his or her God. [2]

These mystic mensches from the Middle Ages were men and women driven healthier, holier, and happier as they drew closer and closer *to the more and more of God*. In joy and sorrow they placed themselves always before the God who cared, and from this overwhelming experience they lived in hope-filled integrity. They have expanded my experience and understanding of God and exposed me to a deeper relationship with the "living something." I believe they will do the same for you when, as I trust, you are moved by their creative energy and their vivid and refreshing descriptions of God's loving work in the world and in your life.

The first mystic I interviewed was Hildegard of Bingen (1098-1179), an energetically assertive and creative woman who has been called the ideal image for the woman of today. This is perhaps why I have chosen to talk with her. As a Benedictine abbess, she was known for her ability to stand strong in an age of unyielding male domination, while expressing her deeply intuitive and artistic nature through writing books on medicine, natural science, prayer, and church politics, as well as writing songs and plays. Hildegard is a mystic firmly planted and blossoming in Mother Earth, a mystic we need to listen to if we are to learn to respect the ground of God on which we tread with seeming indifference.

The second mensch to sit and talk with me was Mechtild of Magdeburg (1210-1280), a woman of some controversy. I chose Mechtild specifically because she was not a cloistered nun and *happily not*. As a layperson, dedicated to the process of religious commitment, she stands out for her devotion to prayer, community living with other women in what has become known as the Beguine movement, and as a radical voice for proper use of the church's financial power for the poor. Mechtild was not a favorite, it seems, of local clergy and bishops who found her alternative lifestyle and criticism threatening.

The third mystic learner of the ways of God was known as

"Teacher." Meister ("master") Eckhart of Hochheim (1260-1328) was a Dominican scholar and very popular preacher. For many years, he served in various leadership roles within his Dominican community, until his elder years when he became entangled in the church's political net of fear. It was at the peak of his illustrious career that the Meister found himself accused of heresy and false teaching, which could have resulted in his excommunication if found to be guilty. Before inquisition boards, bishops, and a pope who seemed bewildered by the imaginative vagueness of his theological thought, the Meister defended his creative use of metaphor and simile in speaking of God. Because Eckhart's God was an eternally creative God of Hope, a youthful God in all, and a God who continually birthed the Word into the world, his spirituality and perspective were received by students and audiences in general as encouragingly positive in an age of bloody wars, physical hardships, and infectious diseases. Perhaps no other medieval mystic can speak so clearly from one age to another as does the Meister. I have interviewed him precisely because so many searching Christians today have found their faith and imagination enflamed by the Meister's energetic and creative God of Compassion.

The fourth spiritually insightful soul of the Middle Ages that I will interview is Jan Van Ruysbroeck (1293-1381), a parish priest, contemplative guide, and author whose spirit was raised by the beauty of his homeland along the Rhine River of Germany. I was inspired to interview this quiet priest by the relatively recent writings of one of the greatest scholars on the subject of mysticism, Evelyn Underhill, who described the gentle Ruysbroeck as the greatest of all mystics. I was also drawn to this holy, human preacher by the fact that, despite his natural inclination toward the quiet of prayer, he frequently felt compelled to speak out with force against what he believed were the outrageous heresies of his day, quietism and pantheism, beliefs that some would consider flourishing still among what have been labeled New Age movements.

The fifth sage of the soul is another mystic of the Rhineland and follower of the great Meister Eckhart, Johannes Tauler (c. 1300-1361). On a personal level, I must say that many of his homilies, thankfully preserved, are some of the most tender and moving sermons I have ever read. No other medieval proclaims the everyday birth of God in the soul with such beautiful strength. As a Dominican preacher, like Eckhart, Johannes Tauler grew in popularity as he preached in almost every church and convent of the German lowlands. As a wandering preacher, his inspiration was, in a sense, as infectious as the plagues that struck so many in his day. The preacher's message, however, enkindled new life, inspiring a movement of spiritual seekers called the "Friends of God."

The sixth mystic I interviewed, although by chance and after some fast talking, is the noted anchoress of the island of England, Julian of Norwich (c. 1342-c. 1431). I was especially interested in meeting this independent and solitary woman because her writings and showings have had a profound impact on one of the greatest of twentieth-century mystics, Thomas Merton. As I drew closer and closer to the Anchorhold in which she lived in almost total solitude for many years, I came to see through her writings that no other mystic in history has captured the beauty and orthodoxy of God as "mother" as splendidly as Julian. I believe you will find this woman of mystery stands equal to many of the noted male mystics of her time, while speaking with relevance to our day.

The seventh and final God-seeker I interviewed on my imaginative travels through the Middle Ages is perhaps the most widely known of the seven mystics interviewed in this book, Teresa of Avila (1515-1582). What drew me to choose Teresa as one of the few mystics I would have a chance to talk with and learn from, was perhaps what drew me in varying degrees to choose all seven for this book, her exceptionally broad vision and resilient faith in the face of seemingly insurmountable odds. With perseverance and insight, Teresa was able not only to reform an entire order of Carmelite nuns and priests so that they would come to flourish and serve throughout the world, but perhaps more courageously inspiring, she was able to grow in spiritual and emotional health through her faith, overcoming what seemed to have been youthful emotional difficulties. Teresa is a wonderful example of the belief that a by-product of seeking God is mental health. With humor and confidence, this Carmelite woman of strength is the only one of these mystics who wrote a detailed autobiography describing her personal transformation before God and others. Perhaps her most famous spiritual writing, however, is *Interior Castles*. This extraordinary book is not a dull classic on the spiritual journey but an enlivening and image-filled description of that journey.

As each of the four women and three male mensches chosen were genuine spiritual guides in their period of history, helping others discover the God of their life and understanding, so they can be again for you today. As models of holy humanness, these daring, innovative, and humble people can help you in your struggles as you live in a struggling world. Although they lived some 400 to 900 years ago, I believe the clarity of their vision can help you, the reader, see God as they saw God, not with their physical eyes, but with eyes that can see in the darkness of life the brightness of God.

So that you may have an opportunity to sample the writings of these mystics, I have, in this revised edition, added several brief excerpts after each interview.

In concluding this introductory letter, let me just make a few very brief remarks about why I chose to use the imaginative format of going back in time to interview, rather than writing what might have been a straightforward, academic study that would perhaps have been better able to nuance some of the details of history, style, influence, language usage as well as theological and philosophical distinctions. To be blunt about it, I did not feel another intricately subtle academic study on mysticism was needed nor did I think you would read it. Mysticism can be at times pretty dull stuff, especially if presented on only an academic level. I hoped this book would challenge, not numb with boredom, to encourage new perspectives and visions, not blind with a complex web of what a good friend calls "theological gobbledygook." I wanted most of all for you, the reader, to meet real people who loved, laughed, hurt, and struggled through life so that you might find the courage to do the same. I did not choose the imaginative interview method with historians and scholars of mysticism in mind as the primary audience, but with you, the reader.

To them I express a clear recognition that what I have undertaken here by way of imagination is certainly hazardous in that I may have mistakenly misrepresented or misinterpreted one or more of the thoughts of these highly esteemed mystics. With one eye on caution, I plunged ahead with deep respect for the full teachings of these seven Western mystics, hoping always that you will be ignited by the spark of their enthusiastic faith.

In the Compassion of Christ,
Rev. John Powers C.P

Hildegard of Bingen
(1098-1179)

This interview took place at dawn on July 19, 1179, in a small cloistered garden beside the Benedictine convent in Rupertsberg, near the present-day village of Bingen, Germany. I had received a written invitation to begin my interviews with the grandmother of the Rhineland mystics, Hildegard of Bingen.

I had been told that despite her eighty years of age and deteriorating health I should be prepared for a lively discussion and if she felt at all inclined a scolding or two from this confident author, poet, playwright, spiritual advisor to popes, archbishops, priests, and nuns, songwriter and student of medicine and natural sciences. I had already read of Hildegard's assertive tendencies when advising church officials or when called into question for her writings and community reforms, so I was not about to be late for my appointment with the abbess.

Our dawn meeting prompted my first question to this creatively influential woman in the history of mysticism. It was a question that rose as the sun through which God burned so brightly for Hildegard.

J.P. Abbess, there are some in my day who have had the opportunity to read your primary writing, *Book of Divine Works*. The general reaction among these people seems to be the belief that your deeply grounded twelfth-century spirituality can be for us of the twentieth century, rolling hopefully into the twenty-first century, a model of living at peace with planet earth. They see in your writings a woman not stuck merely with a God somewhere out in space or imprisoned in the little self we all can be, but they seem to have met in your writings a woman profoundly aware of God's continuous pouring of love into the earth itself.

ABBESS Well, I am not sure whether I am a model for a future time. In fact, what I am is not that important. What is important is who God is for us who call ourselves humans. Human beings must find their right relation in the midst of the world. Among all creatures, human beings are most significant, yet perhaps also the most dependent. We are small in stature really, but in the energy of the soul we are truly powerful.

Our heads may be turned upwards toward God or great thought, but our feet are and must remain on solid ground. All creation is directed for our benefit by God. How can anyone think contrary, especially you, Father, who sit in this rich, green Bavarian garden that has been nourished by the flowing waters of Mother Rhine? All you need do is glance at the sun or look to the moon and stars if you desire to see God's work. Gaze at the beauty of the earth's moist greening and think! What do you see but the joyful delights that God has given as nothing else but gift? God is pouring into creation the love that God is. Is not this gift for the good of all? Do not the earth and stars in all their beauty tell us who God is?

J.P. That is a beautiful affirmation of environmental spirituality, that the earth manifests God. It seems, however, at least in my time, that the most prevalent attitude toward creation, earth, animals, and even other people is one of use and abuse. There is an arrogant dominance over the earth and all creatures that is far more than subduing the earth, but is rather stripping creation of its dignity. I must confess that a more earth-hating attitude has flourished in my age.

ABBESS We should despise only what keeps us from

God, not what points the way to God. Does the earth or its creatures separate me from God, or is it perhaps my own thoughts, actions, or attitudes toward creation that divides?

In reference to creation we believe that God has established the earth and its firmament in wisdom, securing it by the power of the stars. Do you know that there is an ancient agreement between the sun and moon?

J.P. An agreement! You mean a contract?

ABBESS No contract is needed when it is the wisdom of God who promises. You see, Father, it is the sun that lights the moon which then gives light to the stars. Also in this agreement between sun and moon is a vow that the moon will moisten the earth with fruitful rain.

In a manner of speaking, it is creation that clothes God. In this ancient agreement between sun, moon, stars, and earth, we see God. Since God cannot be seen, we know God through what we see. Take for example your body, Father. I cannot see a large part of it because it is clothed, but I know it is there.

J.P. Yes, and more and more of it as I get older, it seems.

ABBESS Beside the point. Just as your clothes garb you, so creation clothes God. The burning brilliance of the sun at its rising speaks of God, as does the greening of the land. This garden of delights in which we sit reveals God. Still the Godhead cannot be seen fully by mortals.

J.P. My period of history seems in sore need of a God who is the greening power of generation. This God of yours is sprouting forth, is one that loves creation and creature as a man and woman love. Yours is a God not of technological dominance but of moistening rain, a God many people in my time are losing touch with as they forget the feel of dirt between their fingers.

ABBESS I am sorry for that. Be sure, however, that God has not lost the touch of greening. It is difficult for us to grasp the abundance of God and creation with our minds. Yet we know, do we not, that the Godhead created all and has formed humanity according to the divine likeness and image?

In one of my earliest visions I was told that God, the highest and fiery power, had kindled every spark of life and emits nothing that is deadly. All reality that is was decided on by

God. With wisdom God put everything in proper order. It is we who do not see the order of the universe yet the fiery life of divine essence makes it so for our benefit. It is God who is aflame beyond the beauty of the meadows, gleams in the waters, burns in the sun, moon, and stars. With every breeze, can you not feel it even now, God awakens life? God remains hidden in every kind of reality as a fiery power.

J.P. To many a Western Christian mind, your description of God sounds almost pagan or at least pantheistic. Do you recommend we worship the trees and rivers, sun and earth?

ABBESS Is there not a difference between worship and reverence? Look my young friend, God is life, entire and whole. God is not struck from stones nor blooming out of the twigs in my garden, nor is God rooted in your power to have children. All life has its roots in God, not the other way around. God is the root; the resounding world blooms out of it, revealing God. All creation therefore has been directed by God the root, to the good of all. If we somehow abuse our position by committing evil deeds, God's judgment will permit other creatures to punish us. If we worship God and reverence all that God gives, using it to praise God, we celebrate goodness, not evil.

J.P. What you seem to be saying is that the world and what's in it is the threshold to and from God. If we worship the earth alone as though it is God, or if we defile and ignore the earth as though it is totally cut off from God, we are locked in the threshold, the doorway to and from God. Stuck in the doorway we go nowhere. Is that right?

ABBESS Perhaps an allegory may be appropriate here. As the word of God penetrates all creation, so the soul, the vital life-force, penetrates the whole body. The soul is the moisture of the body so that it does not dry out, just as rain flows down to quench the earth. When we work in accord with the strivings of the soul, the living breath of God's spirit, all our deeds turn out well. But our deeds turn out ill if we merely follow the strivings of the flesh. The soul and body must work in accord as humanity must work with creation, for God has arranged all things of this world in consideration of everything else. It is the arrogance of the first fallen angel that desires to compete with God, that does not see the light of God as a spark in all creation. Humanity is a spark of God, not the fire itself. God desires the world to be in pure harmony. The earth should not be injured or destroyed. Those with faith direct all their activity toward what God wishes.

J.P. You have a fascinating description of the story of the Fall. It speaks rather pointedly to those of my time who are rather caught up in themselves, who identify with their own self-importance, who have forgotten their place in the scheme of living, desiring to master creation and others.

ABBESS Yes, well, the Fall, as we so politely call it, took place before the beginning of time, which is of course the divine present, when God said, "Let it be done!" All things visible and invisible were then enclosed within their forms, just as the Holy Godhead envisioned them before time was. However, some angels, as some arrogant people, do not wish God to green creation; rather, they would prefer to have control over the power of God and life. Such desire kills life by drying up the moisture of the soul.

J.P. If I may interrupt for a moment, Abbess. As you speak of the Godhead who was before time and who enclosed all forms I cannot help but think of a recent interview with a scholar by the name of Joseph Campbell who spoke of a scientist who called this God the field that produces forms, "the morphogenetic field."

ABBESS "Morphogenetic field" is a rather odd way of speaking about the Godhead who embraces all creation with the royal kiss of love. I understand the use of the term but I cannot imagine being loved by a morphogenetic field. Ultimately, however, the soul knows it comes from its creator. We humans give names to our God, whether as subject or mere object, because the desire to name God is rooted in the good powers of our soul.

J.P. Excuse my interruption. Could you continue with your story of how the angels fell?

ABBESS Yes. Let me add before I do that this story is not only for your age, young priest. It is also for mine, for there are many, clergy included, who rule in such a manner as to oppress the laity by robbery. It is those who seek to make something of themselves who have forgotten that they were created originally as something of God. As there are those men and women today who have forgotten where they stand before God, so before the beginning of time there was a very large choir of angels who sought control and position. It was when they beheld their remarkable glory and their shining beauty in dazzling fullness that they forgot the source of beauty. They had not even begun to praise God when they thought their beauty so powerful that it overshadowed even God's splendor. When, however, they realized that they could never quite outshine the brilliance of God's mysteries they fled in disgust, turning from God. In self-deception they chose another god and therefore were plunged downward into darkness, impotent and dry. Those who contradict the beauty of God's design by refusing to serve in co-creation are deprived of all light. They are blinded by their own darkness.

J.P. So the sin of the angels was to arrogantly want, as some might say in my time, a piece of the rock?

ABBESS Odd expression, but no, they desired to control the rock. It is very much like the ongoing battle in my homeland here along the Rhine River. This is an age of injustice when predatory wolves hunger to feed on what is rightfully another's. There are tyrants who bind heavy loads on the poor and attack church property. There are clergy who wear the mantle of power, ruling estates and farms as though princes. Each social class must have its own integrity, its own piece of the rock as you so state it. Each should glory in its place without robbing from others.

J.P. The class structure of my time is not quite as consciously rigid as yours seems to be; however, sin is the same. Sin is like robbing God of the power to create, claiming that power as your own?

ABBESS Yes, but you cannot steal from God what God is, creative love. God created humanity so that we might cultivate in its broadest sense the earthly, and thereby cultivate the heavenly. God has created me; I have not created God. God is my Lord and has dominion over me. I do not have dominion over God. Through God, I have living spirit, life, movement. It is through God that I learn and find my path. Creation is to be used in God's rhythm.

J.P. When you speak of the earth-creation as kissed by God and call humanity into right relation with the earth, I cannot help but think of what is for my age an old Native American story. Some of your writings would be very much appreciated by these people, despite the fact that their integrity and land have also been the food for hungry wolves. A great man, Chief Seattle, wrote a wonderful letter in 1852 to our leader, whom we call the president, when he was asked to sell tribal lands. The chief wrote in part, "We love this earth as a newborn loves its mother's heartbeat. So if we sell you our land, love it as we love it. Care for it as we care for it. Hold in your mind the memory of the land as it is when you receive it. Preserve the land for all children and love it, as God loves us all. As we are part of the land, so you too are part of the land. The earth is precious to us. Make it precious to you. One thing we know; there is only one God. No man, be he Red Man or White Man, can be apart. We are brothers and sisters after all." [3]

ABBESS With such a love for what has flowed from the Godhead I pray this native man and chief is of the church.

J.P. No, Abbess, he is not.

ABBESS Did your president listen to this wise man's plea?

J.P. Not really, Abbess.

ABBESS The emperors, princes, and popes of my age could learn from such a wise chief. As the letter you shared related, I was told in a vision that the earth is at the same time source and mother. Every holy person draws to themselves all that is earthy. They remain close to creation, for God, through creation, sustains them.

J.P. You have mentioned a few times in our discussion thus far how you have heard something in a vision. Could you tell us what you mean when you say you've had a vision? The reason I ask this is because in my time it seems visions are becoming more common. We have preachers on the airwaves that claim to talk with God, and children in Yugoslavia who claim to see Mary, the Mother of God, as their prayer beads turn to gold. What kind of visions do you have?

ABBESS How can airwaves preach? Of course, you mean this as a metaphor, as the wind whispers of God.

J.P. I'm sorry, Abbess. The airwaves don't preach. I was speaking of the preachers who use what we call television. It's like a talking picture box used for communicating information over many miles.

ABBESS Television. It sounds rather spiritual.

J.P. No, not really. It depends on its use, I guess. Can you speak about your visions?

ABBESS Well, the vision experiences granted to me began when I was a very young girl of perhaps eight years, when God first overshadowed my life. Did you know I was the tenth of ten children? I received my training in the Benedictine life of contemplation when entrusted at age 15 to the hermit Jutta, who was attached to the monastery community of Disibodenberg. Throughout these years at Disibodenberg, where I became abbess at 38 years of age, throughout the difficulties of moving our small women's community of 18 here to Rupertsberg, detaching ourselves from our male brethren, which still causes some irritation, I have experienced visions. I do not fully understand everything I see in these visions, for I remain still in the bondage of this frail body and soul. I still want and suffer because of it. As a matter of fact, I understood from my first vision that I should call my first book, *Scivias*, a book that proclaims the living light.

J.P. How do you see God? Do you envision a physical form or hear an audible voice, or are these a deep intuitive seeing, a creative leap of consciousness to the other side and heart of reality?

ABBESS It seems God endows certain people with insight. From my early childhood when my nerves, limbs, and veins were still weak, the gift of vision brought joy to my soul. This joy remains with me still at 80 years. I do not, however, fall into unconsciousness or ecstasy when seeing, nor do I see what I share in my writings with my external eyes nor hear with my ears. Nor does the gift of vision come from the thoughts of my heart or my emotions, nor are they mediated through my five senses. The light I see is not bound by space. I see under the influence of heavenly mysteries while fully awake and in right mind. I see with the inner eye of my spirit and grasp the sound of reality with the inner ear. I am still a bit uneasy talking about these insights of the soul for I am an uneducated woman and hesitant in the fear that others may not understand. I remained silent about these life-giving sights until I was 40 years old. Then, however, I was persuaded to share these visions by the flashing, shooting, and falling lights that give me, in an instant, all I know of life and God.

J.P. I understand that there were some who were rather critical of your visionary writings.

ABBESS Yes, that is true. I am deeply greatful to the kindness of our Servant Pope Eugenius III, who spoke favorably of my writings.

J.P. I have a remark here from that pope who is quoted as saying at the Council of Trier in 1147, commenting on your visionary abilities, that "so remarkable a lamp should not be put out."

ABBESS God is the light. A lamp is merely the instrument, and I must say God chose a very sickly and dusty lamp through which to brighten a corner of creation.

J.P. Could these visions possibly flow out of your physical ailments? There are some who would evaluate your visions as consistent with psychosomatic illness or even mental illness.

ABBESS I have spent years studying how the humors of the human body are distributed and can be altered by the winds and air. I do not see a conflict of humors as the source of my visions. As I wrote once to Abbot Philip; undoubtedly God has arranged such things to show what the divine can accomplish through a creature that the creature cannot hope to accomplish alone, even from a sickbed of bad humors. I must place all my hope and trust in God alone.

J.P. As you describe your visionary experience, I cannot help but think of a man from the future who spoke of this mystical insight. May I quote him?

ABBESS You have come prepared, that is wise. Please go on.

J.P. The man's name is Albert Einstein, a non-Christian and a genius. He is supposed to have written, "The most beautiful emotion we can experience is the mystical. It is the power of all true art and science. He to whom this emotion is a stranger. . .is as good as dead. To know that what is impenetrable to us really exists, manifesting itself as the highest wisdom and the most radiant beauty, which our dull faculties can comprehend only in their most primitive forms—this knowledge, this feeling, is at the center of true religiousness. In this sense, and in this sense only, I belong to the ranks of devoutly religious men." [4]

ABBESS This man is obviously one who has gone beyond the changing state of the humors into the light that enlivens life.

J.P. You have mentioned the humors within the body a few times. I presume in my language you are speaking of moods.

ABBESS Well, if what you call moods change because thoughts change, at times savagely attacking us from within like a leopard, while at other times becoming moderate like a crab that crawls, then moods and humors are the same. At times the humors, or moods as you say, lull us into confidence and then plunge us again into confusion. Often they may guide us upward into the proper spirit of reverence from which the power of justice flows. It is when our contradictory humors and thoughts give rise to an uproar that they confuse the soul to the point that it no longer listens, recognizes what is good, and creatively does what is just.

J.P. What is it, Abbess, that reconciles the conflicting thoughts, moods or humors so that a person is liberated and finds peace?

ABBESS It is the Living Light. When and how I see it, I cannot express; but for the time I do see it, all sadness and anguish are taken from me. It is then that I have the air of an innocent young girl rather than a little old woman.

J.P. Is our task then to seek to live in the light that you experience? Is that what you do, always seek to contemplate the light?

ABBESS A believing person should always be about directing themselves and others to God. Our human task has two aspects: to sing the praises of God and to do the good works of God. Through praise God is made known, while through good works and justice the wonders of God can be seen. The hallmark of humanity is the doing of good works.

The work of God is brought to its fullness in humanity. The human species has within its soul the ability to arrange everything according to its own wish; hopefully in right relation with God, the divine origin of all creation. If you are in right relation with God, so too are you in proper relations with all creatures. You are a person who is just to all. It is then that the light of God shines in and about you. Can there be any greater peace than to know one lives in the light and reflects on others the very brightness of God?

J.P. As we conclude this all-too-brief interview, let me ask about something, or actually someone, who is not mentioned in many of the introductions or summaries to your spiritual writings, and whom you have not mentioned in our interview. We have talked about the Divine Living Light of God who creates in germinating love. What of Jesus?

ABBESS My young man, first, you did not ask me directly about Jesus. It was, however, most appropriate to begin this dawn discussion with visions of creation. That is where Scripture begins. Our spiritual lives and thoughts should begin where Scripture does, should they not? However, we have truly been talking of Jesus all along. I have spoken of the Word who dwelt in God eternally, who in the fullness of grace created the cosmos in divinity and redeemed it through humanity. The Word accepted this flesh just as our blood vessels support and cover our bodies and carry our blood. The blood vessels are not the blood itself but they carry the blood flow from source to extremities. So the flesh carries the Word of God, Jesus the begotten Son. It pleased God to adopt the garment of human flesh; the Word and the flesh formed a united life. The Word and flesh are one within the unity of a person. As the body is the garment of the Word of Jesus, so the body conceals and reveals our soul. Our bodies would be nothing without the soul, and our soul could do nothing without the body. The arrangement creates oneness. The Word is not diminished in divinity as a result of the flesh; rather, the flesh is made the garment of God.

J.P. I have recently heard the scholar Joseph Campbell, an expert in comparative religion and mythology, refer to you as a great female saint of the Middle Ages. You have been a

Benedictine for over 70 years and an abbess in the structured Benedictine community for over 40 years. You've written books: *Scivias*, which means "Know the Way," *The Book of Life's Merits*, and *The Book of Divine Works*. You've studied medicine and the physical sciences producing handbooks on health and what we might call first aid. You've also written about the lives of significant saints, Disibode, Rupert, and Benedict, and you have written many very beautiful songs, which are being reproduced in my time, and if that's not enough you have had regular correspondence with popes and bishops on issues of great personal and institutional concern. I understand that at one point in your career as a religious superior there was the possibility of excommunication from the church if you did not follow the demands of the church officials. Quite obviously you are a strong woman of considerable creative insight and perception. My question, however, is this. Few of us have the depth of insight you have or the vocation to the contemplative life that God gave you. Most of us are ordinary people without church position or theological knowledge, and most are married. What do your visions mean to an ordinary person?

ABBESS I consider myself excessively ordinary, yet I live to praise God through creation. Thank you for all the compliments and for embarrassing me with a list.

Before I answer your question by making some remarks to those people you call ordinary, let me say something about a phrase you used that surprised me. You said this Mr. Campbell called me the "female saint of the Middle Ages."

J.P. Yes.

ABBESS Well, God will decide the issue of saintliness, but the stunning remark you made was to describe my time in history as the Middle Ages. I have seen visions of the end times. It will be an epoch filled with disturbances and constant upheavals. Perhaps it is because my own ending draws near that I see signs of the end times all about me, in the oppression of people, faith, and creation. I never thought that we were merely in the Middle Ages of history, however, and that many new sprouts will shoot up for years to come. What surprised me is that you described my time as the Middle Ages. It seems this changing world has a long way to go.

J.P. Some people in my time as well, Abbess, see signs of the end of the earth because of ozone depletion, pollution buildup, and nuclear threat. As in your time so in mine, I hope, there will be many new sprouts of possibility that will blossom.

ABBESS Strange words you use: ozone, nuclear. I do not know what they mean, but let me answer your original question. Let me speak to those people you have called ordinary, who in many respects are bound more than all clergy to praise God and serve justice. It is the task of those who marry to adhere to God's command of love; the task of those who work to build up and cultivate the earth so that the needed fruit and wine may be provided for nourishment. It is the task of parents to care for their children in an environment of love rather than in a poisonous atmosphere.

No one—clergy, religious, or laity—can cast off the regulation and discipline of God's law. Do not forget it is God who gives us all that we have: children, farmlands, sheep, cattle, livestock, and our possessions. It is the Radiant Light and Creator who has at daybreak on the first day of creation planted in our hearts the very power of generation.

J.P. Your writings have much to say to those who struggle to live peacefully in my twentieth century. I thank you for the opportunity to talk.

ABBESS I will pray, Father John, that the living light will continue to shine in your time of history; that your age, too, may be one day called "middle."

Abbess Hildegard of Bingen died 810 years ago at Rupertsberg on the Rhine on September 17, 1179. As she was profoundly influential in her age so she seems to have found a new birth today among those who seriously seek after God. No canonization process was ever completed by the Roman Catholic church, but she is listed as a saint in the Roman List of Martyrology and is devoutly revered in parts of Germany.

Suggested Readings

Book of Divine Works with Letters and Songs, by Hildegard of Bingen, ed. Matthew Fox. Santa Fe, N.M.: Bear & Co., 1987.

Meditations with Hildegard of Bingen, by Gabriele Uhlein. Santa Fe, N.M.: Bear & Co., 1983.

Silent Fire: An Invitation to Western Mysticism, ed. Walter Holden Capps and Wendy M. Wright. San Francisco: Harper & Row, 1978.

Excerpts
from the writings of
HILDEGARD OF BINGEN

"For everything I had written in my earlier visions and came to know later I say under the influence of heavenly mysteries while my body was fully awake and while I was in my right mind. I saw it with the inner eye of my spirit and grasped it with my inner ear. In this connection I was never in a condition similar to sleep, nor was I ever in a state of spiritual rapture, as I have already emphasized in connection with my earlier visions."

Book of Divine Works, Foreword

"God had directed for humanity's benefit all of creation, which God has formed both on the heights and in the depths. If we abuse our position to commit evil deeds, God's judgment will permit other creatures to punish us."

Book of Divine Works, Vision Three, 2

"For just as the word of God has penetrated everything in creation, the soul penetrates the whole body in order to have an affect on it. The soul is also the moisture of the body because the soul moistens it so that it does not dry out, just as rain flows down into the Earth...."

Book of Divine Works, Vision Four, 21

"Thus the soul, which is moderated by wisdom, saturates human beings with the waters of a gushing stream, which is God."

Book of Divine Works, Vision Four, 81

"Without woman, man could not be called man; without man, woman could not be named woman....Neither of them could henceforth live with the other."

Book of Divine Works, Vision Four, 100

"For there are concealed in all of nature—in the animals, reptiles, birds and fishes as well as in the plants and fruit trees—certain hidden mysteries of God which no human being and no other creature can know or feel unless this is especially granted by God."

Book of Divine Works, Vision Four, 105

"...what should occur in the total fullness of creation. It is, so to speak, the greening power of generation in a shoot as it sprouts forth."

Book of Divine Works, Vision Ten, 2

"In no way has God ordered that a cloak and a mantle should be given to one son while another goes naked."

Book of Divine Works, Vision Ten, 16

Mechtild of Magdeburg
(c. 1210 - c. 1283)

On July 21, 1270, as dusk whispered across the low country of southern Thuringia, I met with Mechtild of Magdeburg in a simple, stone Cistercian chapel attached to a convent at Helfa in Saxony, a village between present-day Leipzig to the south and Magdeburg, Germany, to the north.

I had been informed that I was to meet with a woman of some 60 years who had only recently moved to the Helfa Cistercian convent after living many years in an alternative community of women in Magdeburg. I was also informed that Mechtild was a woman of some notoriety in Magdeburg for her radical criticism of the clergy's use of money and influence and for her daringly imaginative book entitled, *The Flowering Light of the Godhead.* At 23 years of age, Mechtild, the daughter of a noble family, had chosen to enter, not a convent or cloister, but to gather with other women into what we might call a base community whose purpose was to provide an atmosphere of sharing, prayer, and support for the charitable work the women would do. It had been a fast-growing concept of communal living with thousands in scattered gatherings throughout Thuringia, but it had not been accepted well by some official clergy. Because of her involvement in what has come to be called the Beguine movement, her outspoken views concerning the clergy and her extraordinary writing, Mechtild, I was told, felt it best to move out of Magdeburg for a time. Some say she was practically forced to flee by local priests, run out on a rail, so to speak. This prompted my first question.

J.P. Lady Mechtild, first, thank you for the opportunity to talk with you briefly about your spiritual experiences, your book, and your insights into the religious movements of your day.

LADY M. It is my honor. Since my recent departure from Magdeburg, I have not shared much with friends other than the sisters here at Helfa. I thank God for these friends, especially for Gertrude and Mechtild, for their sisterly concern and their invitation to make my home with them.

J.P. Can you tell us, if it is not too painful, why you were in a manner forced to leave Magdeburg where you had lived for so long, doing good work out of your community of Beguines?

LADY M. I'm sorry, but perhaps you do not know that to refer to our gathering of women in Magdeburg as a Beguine community is somewhat offensive. I have only recently heard that term applied to the perhaps hundreds of large and small communities of women who have chosen to live together for religious and charitable reasons outside the usual church structure of contemplative cloistered life. The term "Beguines" is a mocking term used by some clergy who associate our movement with a touch of heresy. Our movement of laity has caused some controversy since we are not under the direct control of the priests and bishops. Some clergy are so threatened by our alternative lifestyle that they make us out to be enemies of the church, which we're truly not. I deeply love my Catholic tradition. I only pray that we work harder to reform some of our unjust and oppressive ways.

J.P. I am sorry I used what is for us an historical phrase that lumps all of your spiritual-based communities together. History tends to merely throw people into categories without deference at times to the heart of the matter. I must say your movement of, what shall we call it, "gatherings," is not unusual for my time either. We have had men and women come together in what we have called communes, some with healthy religious motivation and others with rather destructive reasons. We now have a concept called "Christian base communities," which I think comes close to your movement in Magdeburg. I gather then that you would have preferred to have stayed in Magdeburg?

LADY M. Yes, I would have, but the tension grew too much for me. I found that unbelief almost surrounded me as the fighting for position of control and authority went on among clergy and bishops who wished to restrict our movement for their own comfort. We wished an independence the church would not allow, so legislation flowed easily from the hands of local clergy frightened of our piety and popularity among the people. I also found it very difficult to bear the thought that some few would think my writings, which were faithfully encouraged by the gifted Dominican Heinrich of Halle, would be suspect in regards to faith. I am not a theologian but I do not believe my writings are offensive to our Lord in any way. They are what the Lord has opened to me.

J.P. I am not here to judge the clergy, Lady Mechtild, but you still seem rather hurt by what has happened.

LADY M. I am. I do not wish to speak from self-pity. It is very unlike me to do so. I am sad to see what seems like the beginning of the end of a beautiful spiritual movement among the women of my lovely city, Magdeburg. We have few options to express our deep spiritual love except to enter a sanctioned cloister, and we wished to share our work with oppressed peoples more than convent life would allow. What is happening in the church among my friends causes me great suffering. Under the advice of my long-time and cherished spiritual friend, Father Heinrich of Halle, I chose to leave Magdeburg and my gathering to seek to understand what this poverty, pain, and emptiness will teach me. I have in this school of suffering complained at times to the Lord that the rejection and mistrust that encircled me in Magdeburg was too heavy a burden for me. There were even moments, and at times they rise up still, that I wonder how long I must remain here on earth in this mortal body as a target at which people throw stones, offending my honor. I have felt the shock of evil cunning. The light of my lantern has flickered at such pain.

J.P. And how has the Lord responded to your complaint of suffering?

LADY M. Oh, the Lord replies so evenly as a physician who brings healing ointment for the wounds. It is the Living Spark, Soaring Eagle, and Cooling Stream of God who promises to take this burden from me, embracing it to himself so that I may more easily carry it.

J.P. So when you cry out to God that life is too difficult, or that your loneliness too great, or your sufferings too heavy to carry God does not merely take them all away? Your remarks remind me of the line: "Life is not so much a test, but rather a teacher who gives us more to learn when we have yet not learned enough from the previous lessons."

LADY M. No. The Lord does not merely take the pain away, but rather has given me the power to change my ways. It is the Divine Love that is so immensely great that it overflows; it ceaselessly pours itself out into my small vessel of a soul and body, even to overflowing. When I can no longer bear the hurt, loneliness, or suffering I must, as you must, share it with some of God's friends. I have told my spiritual counselor and my sisters that I too suffer. In this way we are in longing together, sighing to be in union with the Godhead.

J.P. So suffering has taught you something?

LADY M. I've learned this from suffering. You will never be made complete in God unless you embrace your wounds in love. Let me tell you a tale of how Pain once rose from the body and soul like a dark cloud and traveled to God and in a loud voice said, "Lord, you know what I want." The Lord, of course, met Pain at the gates of the kingdom and said in reply, "I know you, Pain; welcome. I wore you as a robe on my body when living on earth. The hatred of the world was my cloak. No matter how prized and valuable you were there on earth, however, you cannot enter the kingdom. You must return to your maid." The Lord then went on to tell Pain to be a messenger to me, "and tell her that I will do two things for her if she will do two for me. First, she must be modest and second, wise. Then I shall first embrace her and second take her to my heart in union." Then Pain complained to the Lord, in defense, "I make many people holy. I nourish them and bring them to heaven, even though I myself am not holy or evil and can never get into heaven." The Lord then answered Pain by saying, "Pain, you were not born in heaven, therefore you cannot get in. You were born out of the heart of Lucifer, so you must return to live there forever."

Do you see, Father John, that pain is a teacher? If we can accept it as part of life we can learn prudence and wisdom; we can rise up. That is why even God took this human path, one marked by the most deep suffering and pain. In so doing, God shows us the way to be holy and noble. We must all remember that when our Easter comes, and it will, God will be all around us, through us, giving us ultimate love.

J.P. So it is the love of God, the embrace and taking in of God that helps you place pain and suffering in its proper place and perspective? You had to embrace your love for the church, for example, a love which wounded you in Magdeburg.

LADY M. Yes, but love always secretly flows from God into the soul and draws us back to its source. To put it another way, fish don't drown in the water, gold does not disappear in the fire, nor do birds fall naturally from the sky. What God gives to all creatures is to seek their own nature. How do I find my nature? Through God, humanity, and love. I am truly God's forever no matter what the pain.

J.P. Now you've hit on a point that struck me earlier on in our conversation. You believe, I think, that the greatest wound of love is to experience an absence or separation from God. Is that right?

LADY M. Yes. To be surrounded by the dark, cut off from the flowing light of the Godhead, would cause the greatest distress and longing of all. Such a darkness could cause one to lose the light and consciousness of God's intimate love for you. Even if all the mountains flowed with healing ointment, and all the waters contained healing powers, and all the forests and flowers dripped with the oil of joy, it would never be enough to recover from the absence of God. The bride of the soul longs always for union with the Lord. God never has enough intercourse with the soul, and we can never have enough of God.

J.P. The way you speak about loving God with such expressionistic and almost sensual images, I can't help but think of a story from Persia about a mutual acquaintance you mentioned earlier, Lucifer. The story goes, as I am told, that Satan was once the greatest of angels, loving God more than any other angel. Satan and the angels bowed only to God as God had instructed them at their creation. As it happened God then decided to create the universe, earth, stars, light, creatures of all kinds, and humanity whom God decided would be a higher form in his hierarchy than the angels. God then asked the angels to serve human beings. Satan absolutely refused. He would bow to no one but God as he had been earlier instructed. His egotistical love for God prevented him from serving the humans God had made. Satan was indignant that God would change his mind, placing humans over angels. Satan insisted that he would only serve and love God, so God had no choice but to cast Lucifer out of heaven for refusing to love who God loved. There are a number of points one could draw from this story, but the one I wish to refer to is that from this story hell becomes the absence of the one whom Satan passionately and egotistically loves more than any other, God. Although Satan's love is self-centered, the story makes your point, Lady Mechtild, that to be separated from the one you love is the greatest of human pains.

LADY M. Yes. In pride I can so easily lose God, in sin I climb the highest mountain that places distance between my soul and God. I believe and have learned in the darkness of my anguish that from the beginning God captured and bound me; that the Trinity gave itself into creation, made me and you, body and soul, all out of infinite love. All was fashioned most nobly. Love itself flows from God into us without effort or work. It moves like a bird gliding smoothly without beating the air. God has given himself completely to me with all his creatures. What can I do but sink into thankfulness. There are many kinds of storms in this world, but then the sun shines. Love transforms the empty heart even when we must struggle through hardship and pain. When you lie down in the fire of God, you can taste the flowing Godhead through your very being. You can feel the Spirit driving and moving you into the light and flowing fire of God.

J.P. Not long ago I interviewed an abbess by the name of Hildegard. She spoke most frequently of God as the light of life that shines as the sun at daybreak. You speak of this light of God as a fire that also shines, yet burns as well. Fire may be necessary, but it does burn.

LADY M. Now I have a story for you. There was this poor fellow who was thinking simply about God's great nobility. He stood in awe of God. God then showed him in the eyes of his soul, a fire which continually burned high above all things. It had burned from the beginning and would burn without end. The fire itself is the ever-living God from which all things proceed. The sparks of this fire which have blown away from the fire are the angels. The beams of the fire are the saints who shine their light on Christianity. The coals and embers of this fire still glow; they are the just who here on earth burn in God's heavenly love while enlightening us by their good works. If these good people are chilled by sin, they can warm themselves by the coals that remain hot. The crackling sparks that are reduced to ashes when thrown from the fire are the bodies of those blessed people who have died, yet await their heavenly reward. Finally, in our story we have the Lord of the Fire, Jesus Christ, who shall on the last day gather all of the sparks of the fire to fashion a wondrous chalice for God who, on the day of his eternal marriage will drink with Jesus all the holiness he has poured into our senses and souls.

J.P. What, Lady, of those who refuse to love, who are, as you put it, "chilled" by sin?

LADY M. They have cursed themselves by not longing and hungering for God enough to love others, too. They perhaps have become bound to things or refuse to drink the waters of sorrow or to love all things in God. God is the sun, I a reflection. If I refuse to be a mirror reflection of the light of compassion, I depart from God into never-ending emptiness. For such people we must have compassion for they stand without God.

J.P. To change the subject a bit, Lady Mechtild, I would like to return to an earlier part of our discussion where we talked about what seems to have been primarily a women's movement of communal spiritual living.

LADY M. Yes, I often refer to this as the desert way. Others call us the cloaked women because of our rather ordinary dress and the mantle many of us wear.

J.P. I see. Why is it, Lady, that you chose not to enter a convent or cloister, there to pray always in the fire of contemplation?

LADY M. I chose a life of chastity, poverty, and religious devotion but desired also to lead a life of apostolic compassion. I do not judge those who chose the life of a cloister convent; in fact, I stand by them, for many are spiritual friends. To me and many other women, God's love bid us to the desert of work. Whoever wishes to follow God in good and honest work cannot stand still but must travel on. I move on to vanquish evil spirits, to give equally to friend and enemy in need, to seek out and comfort the stranger, prisoner, and those who are ill and poor. The spirit of God is compassion pouring from Father and Son into my poor soul and body. When we on earth then pour out God's mercy and compassion from our hearts, perhaps by dedicating ourselves to the service of the broken, we then, to the degree that we pour out resemble, reflect, and mirror the Holy Spirit, the fire and light of God. We are most like God when we practice what God practices in us, justice and compassion. To answer your question as to why I joined the holy women in Magdeburg, perhaps it was to stand by others with God. When you do this, people open themselves to you and God.

J.P. Since you told a story, may I tell just one more? It speaks to your point about compassionate living.

LADY M. Our time draws short. The nuns here will soon have evening prayer, but please go on with your story.

J.P. I am not sure where I heard this tale, but it is of a young man who in his late teen years felt overwhelmed by guilt. He judged himself as uncaring and selfish, and he did not believe himself fit for human company. In order not to be harmful and offensive to others all his life he thought quite seriously of living his entire life in seclusion, cut off from all people. After much reflection and after consulting a wise guide he decided to commit himself to the community in which he resided and to act as if he really loved them, as though he cared.

For the rest of his long life he gave himself to respecting the rights of others. He was devoted to living a life of tender justice no matter how he felt about himself or others. Over the years, of course, many people came to love him dearly. On his deathbed finally, old and feeble as he was, he decided to confess to all present that his supposed love, concern, and care was a show, merely a mask he wore to hide the true selfishness that lived within him.

To the people sitting with him, this was a deep shock for they held this man up as one beloved. Now at the hour of his death to hear him say that his years of compassion were all a fraud caused them great anguish and tears. God, however, smiled.

LADY M. For that young man the fire burned, drawing him to the compassion of God. In my old age I find myself more prone to criticize. The young man of your story at least did not deceive himself. I find those who try to storm the heavenly heights with fierceness and ascetical practices to be grim of heart and lacking humility. The young man of your story was humble enough to know that through him compassion could reveal itself.

J.P. You may have many years here at Helfa with your spiritual sisters. Years that may bring a greater peace.

LADY M. Old age can be cold, graceless, and powerless. Every little ill seems to bring an impatience that is hardly noticed in youth. A good old age demands patient waiting and trust in God alone. I shall continue to make use of everything that comes my way, welcoming all as best as I am able. I shall attempt to bear the adversity that comes, dwelling always by the comfort of the fire. And I shall plead.

J.P. Plead! Plead for what?

LADY M. I plead to the Lord Pilgrim as I did in a vision some years ago. One night I saw the Lord Jesus dressed as a pilgrim. It seems he had been wandering all through Christendom. I fell down at his feet and said, "Lord Pilgrim, from where have you come?" He answered, "From Jerusalem," which of course meant the Holy Church. He went on to say that he had been driven out of his dwelling, complaining that the heathens did not know him, the Jews did not want him, and the Christians were striving to overthrow him. I pleaded with the Lord Pilgrim for the community, world, and church that we be given another chance. The Lord Pilgrim continued to lament that even after all he had done from the beginning and after all he had suffered, he could no longer find anyone on whom he could pour out his loving grace. He complained even further, raging that "People have driven me out of even their hearts by their self-will so I promise, if I can find no resting place in them I shall abandon them to their arrogance. Then when they die, I shall judge them as I find them then." As I pleaded years ago, young priest, so I plead now as I sit by the comfort of the Pilgrim's fire. Dear Lord, let us not perish. I, Lord Pilgrim, will set a light in the churchyard by which people may come to know themselves.

Mechtild of Magdeburg died at the Cistercian convent at Helfa in Thuringia after many years of chronic illness and blindness. The movement of women mockingly called Beguines had many stormy years before being censured by the Catholic church, being permanently forbidden by some church documents, persecuted by others, and finally being vaguely tolerated in the fifteenth century. The wisdom and orthodoxy of a mystic like Mechtild cannot be overshadowed, however, by politics within the structure of the church regarding alternative community living. Although never canonized, this laywoman of the thirteenth century was regarded as a saint by her contemporaries. Today, Mechtild is highly praised as a vividly imaginative incarnation theologian.

Suggested Readings

The Revelation of Mechtild of Magdeburg or The Flowering Light of the Godhead. trans. Luch Menzies. London: Longmans, Green & Co., 1953.

Meditations with Mechtild of Magdeburg, by Sue Woodruff. Santa Fe, N.M.: Bear & Co., 1982.

Excerpts from the writings of MECHTILD OF MAGDEBURG

"When your Easter comes, I shall be all around you. I shall be through and through you, and I shall steal your body and give you to your Love."

The Revelation of Mechtild of Magdeburg, Book One, 3

"Those who would storm the heavens by fierceness and ascetic practices deceive themselves badly. Such people carry grim hearts within themselves, they lack true humility which alone leads the soul to God."

The Revelation of Mechtild of Magdeburg, Book Two, 1

"I who am Divine am truly in you. I can never be sundered from you; however far we are parted, never can we be separated. I am in you and you are in me. We could not be any closer. We two are fused into one, poured into a single mould, thus unwearied, we shall remain forever."

The Revelation of Mechtild of Magdeburg, Book Two, 25

"I will draw my breath and your soul shall come to me as a needle to a magnet."

The Revelation of Mechtild of Magdeburg, Book Five, 158

"Power is made for service. I am your servant; I am not your master."

The Revelation of Mechtild of Magdeburg, Book Six, 1

"Do not judge others. Stand by them with love. Then God will lead them to be open with you."

The Revelation of Mechtild of Magdeburg, Book Six, 1

"When we on earth pour out compassion and mercy from the depths of our hearts and give to the poor and dedicate our bodies to the service of the broken, to that very extent do we resemble the Holy Spirit who is a compassionate out-pouring of the Creator and the Son."

The Revelation of Mechtild of Magdeburg, Book Six, 32

"In so far as we love compassion and practice it steadfastly, to that extent do we resemble the heavenly Creator who practices these things ceaselessly in us."

The Revelation of Mechtild of Magdeburg, Book Six, 32

"Our childhood was foolish, our youth troubled. Alas! Now, in my old age I find much to criticize, for it can produce no shining work; it can be cold and without grace. Life appears powerless now that it no longer has youth to help it endure the fiery love of God. It is impatient—little ills afflict it much which in youth it noticed hardly at all. Yes, a good old age must be full of patient waiting and trust in God alone."

The Revelation of Mechtild of Magdeburg, Book Seven, 3

"...make our souls a cradle and lay the Beloved there with joyful and loving hearts offering Him praise and glory."

The Revelation of Mechtild of Magdeburg, Book Seven, 21

"Great is the overflow of Divine Love for it is never still. Always ceaselessly and tirelessly it pours itself out, so that the small vessel which is ourselves might be filled to the brim and might also overflow."

The Revelation of Mechtild of Magdeburg, Book Seven, 55

Meister Eckhart of Hochheim
(c.1260 - c.1328)

In the late evening of an early December day in 1326, I arrived in Cologne, a large city of Roman origin that had almost 100 churches by the time Meister Eckhart, the scholarly Dominican preacher from the Erfrut area of Germany, had arrived in 1322 to teach at the university.

Despite his 66 years of age, the Meister had granted permission for my interview after having checked my credentials thoroughly. I was not surprised also that the Meister wanted a commitment of confidentiality since he was embroiled at the time of the interview in a controversy regarding some of his teachings that could cause, if handled carelessly, censure, or even, God forbid, excommunication.

When I met the young student, Heinrich Suso, in front of the large Dominican church to be escorted through the priory to the calefactory, or warming room, to meet the Meister, I could tell by his manner that Heinrich was a bit suspicious of my purpose. After assuring him of my high esteem for what the Meister had preached and written, he relaxed enough to share some priory gossip about a recent meeting the Meister and Nicholas of Strasbourg, the Vicar General of the German Province, had had with the three inquisitors who were conducting the investigation into the Meister's work. It seemed that during the formal questioning by the investigators the Meister had clearly embarrassed them by reminding them often that they seemed to be confused about what was or was not orthodox church teaching. The proceedings against the Meister were not going well as far as the aged Franciscan Archbishop of Cologne, Heinrich of Virneburg, was concerned. The archbishop was determined that the Dominican influence would be stamped out one way or another. These were dangerous days for a popular preacher and teacher, especially one of the Meister's intellect and imagination.

The course to the Meister's study cell near the library seemed to take forever as we walked the cold stone halls and steps of this large priory. Once there, however, and once introduced by young Heinrich to the great teacher, I immediately made mention of my sorrow at his present tense relationship with the local archbishop, and added the promise that I would not presume to question him on matters that were being investigated as...heretical. The Meister spoke right up.

MEISTER Sit down, young priest. I have been at meetings all day on foolish matters. Now it seems they are attempting to defame my superior and friend, Nicholas, as though he were a heretic for coming to my aid. Perhaps this is the archbishop's way of punishing me for preaching in September against these whole proceedings. I have said over and over that I never was nor am I now a willful heretic against the teachings of the church, nor do I believe that anything I have preached or written is heresy. If someone can prove that my teaching is incorrect, I will recant that teaching. I am not, however, a heretic.

J.P. What did you preach in September that may have

caused the archbishop's retaliation against you?

MEISTER I simply stated, perhaps with a bit too much thunder, that if I were any less famous as a preacher and if I had a bit less fervor for justice, I am sure that I would not have false accusations brought against my preaching and teaching by envious men. The entire procedure against me is illegal and unjust and is both time-consuming and frustrating. I was assigned here to teach our young students in the general studies program at the university, not to spend all my time defending myself against misrepresented statements about me.

Excuse me, Father John, but it becomes more difficult each day to retain my peace of mind and composure. I try to remind myself in prayer that God is goodness and remains ever so, no matter how we try to move him to perform this or that deed. God wants us to forget the notion that our deeds move him to give us what we want. Among the multitude of God's gifts I am not important. I try today, and I will tomorrow and every day, to empty myself so as to build my life upon God alone. In such nakedness peace will be born as it will be again at the end of this cold Advent season. Thank the goodness of God for this warming fire, eh, Father?

J.P. Yes, Meister. The fire is indeed helpful. Perhaps during these days of turmoil it might be consoling to remember your colleague in theology, the great Doctor Thomas Aquinas. He was exonerated of false teachings and canonized only three short years ago by the very same pope you prepare to appeal to with your case, John XXII.

MEISTER As I studied my brother Thomas in life, so now I pray for his strength and saintliness. If, however, a Meister must go through this kind of turmoil to become a saint, Lord, save me from saintliness. Perhaps I should make a public statement of some sort to try to clear the air. These are very troublesome times, Father.

J.P. There is a saying of the East, Meister, that claims the job of the orthodox community, the institutional church, is to give the mystic exactly what he or she wants which is, of course, union with God. It seems, as far as the institution is concerned, the quickest route to that union is through mortification and death.

MEISTER The quickest way to God is to let God be all in all. Sadly so many perform their work in order to go to heaven. We are on the wrong track. Until we learn to work without a why, we have not learned to live. So many try to love God like they love a cow, for its milk and cheese or for the profit they will gain. Whether we love God for outward riches or for inner comfort, it is the same principle. Those who do not love God correctly, merely love for their own advantage.

J.P. You said your age is troublesome, Meister. In what ways is it so, other than the fact that the institutional church seems to be showing its uglier political side right now?

MEISTER First, let me say something of our wondrous Creator. Are we not all still in the process of being born? God creates all but does not stop creating. God forever creates. The Is-ness that is God continues to become. God is eternally young and will make all things new again, even through times of darkness. You ask me what troubles have flourished in my age. We have seen violence against popes; heretics are abused by the self-righteous; the pope has had to remain in Avignon, France, because of power struggles with emperors and kings who demand control over the church's vast lands and wealth. The weak arrogance of men has indeed held sway as people starve in my Rhine homeland where there are too many mouths to feed. There have been upheavals in almost every major city, which threatens to tear our church apart. The excess and violence of thought and teaching are unbelievable, while God-searching people are crudely treated by bishops who have merely purchased their positions of power. There is a great fear and despair in the land. Wealth, advantage, and power are born ugly in these dark times.

J.P. As you speak, Meister, I cannot help but compare your period of history with my own. You mention corruption in high places, population growth with famine as a result, floods, a real disillusionment with structures and a sense of hopelessness. Perhaps, Meister, this sense of fear is why your message of new birth is popular both in your time as in mine. Your powerful sermons have deeply touched me, especially your image of pregnancy and birth.

MEISTER The Word of God is a hidden Word and comes in the darkness of night. The birth of God takes place in darkness. Just as Bethlehem was dark on the eve of Christ's birth, so it is still. It seems darkness continues even in your time, Father John. Not only is the Son of the heavenly Creator born in this darkness; but you, too, Father John, are born there as a child of the very same heavenly Creator. What in truth is your name? Is it John? No! What is my name? Eckhart? No! Our name is that we must be born. And what is the Creator's name? To bear. To generate. To give birth. Every creature—you, John, and I—are a word of God, a book about God. It is as though God lies in a maternity bed like a woman, giving birth into every good soul that abandons its selfishness and receives the indwelling God. Let me tell you of a man who had a dream. In it he dreamt that even though a man, he was pregnant. He was full of the nothingness, pregnant like a woman with child. In this dream God was born out of this nothingness.

J.P. I have heard of this dream before, Meister. Some think you are the man in the dream, pregnant with God.

MEISTER Some things are meant for silence. What is important, however, is that life flows out of this Godhead. Every creature is full of God, pregnant unto birth.

J.P. Meister, it seems in one breath you speak about the darkness and threat that shadow our similar times, while speaking also with exuberance about this God who is being born. In the darkness you find the joy of God. How?

MEISTER I find God to be like someone who would hide in the dark, yet who loudly clears his throat in order to give his presence away. God hides in waiting, waiting to give us love; not only waiting but acting, speaking, pouring out. All creatures flow out of God, yet remain within. Creation does not stand outside of God, nor alongside, nor beyond. All created things are in God's circle so that they may flow out and return. Such knowledge should give us all joy, an exuberance that fills the land. Just as God laughed and begot the Son, then together Jesus and the Father laughed and begot the Spirit, so we must laugh so that God is born in us and in our darkened world.

J.P. Meister, before you go any further, I can't help but share something from a Meister of my time. It captures for me this sense of exuberance at discovering God in the dark. The teacher's name is Walter Burghardt. He writes, "Let me make an uncommonly honest confession. In the course of half a century, I have seen more Catholic corruption than you have read of. I have tasted it. I have been reasonably corrupt myself.

"And yet," now here, Meister, is God clearing his throat or being born in Burghard: "I joy in this church—this living, pulsing, sinning people of God. I love it with a crucifying passion. Why? For all the Catholic hate, I experience here a community of love. For all the institutional idiocy, I find here a tradition of reason. For all the individual repressions, I breathe here an air of freedom. For all the fear of sex, I discover here the redemption of my body. In an age so inhuman, I touch here the tears of compassion. In a world so grim and humorless, I share here rich joy and earthy laughter. In the midst of death, I hear here an incomparable stress on life. For all the apparent absence of God, I sense here the real presence of Christ." [5]

MEISTER That is the statement of a just and noble soul, one who has let go so that God can be God in him. He is indeed a royal child of God. The spring of God flows up through this man's soul. He has been hooked by God's love for him and all creation. I have long thought, John, that love is very much like a fishhook. Someone fishing will not catch a fish unless the fish first takes the hook. If the fish takes the hook, no matter how hard it may try to get away, fighting and squirming, the fisher is sure to catch it. Love is the same way. It is forever seeking to capture us as it certainly has the Meister you have just quoted. He has been caught for sure. No matter who it is, whether noble, king, poor man, child, man or woman, whoever is captured by the hook of love belongs to God. The whole person's hands, mouth, feet, eyes, and heart are God's. Look for God's hook and you will be joyfully caught. To be caught by God is to be caught by freedom. The Meister you quoted is free from all that might hook him into anger, jealousy, envy, greed for power, and ultimately death. He is free to swim in the ocean of God.

J.P. Fish stories seem to run among those inclined toward God. There is an Indian priest who has translated a story from the East that tells of a young fish who is continually asking an older fish where the ocean is.

MEISTER We are in the ocean of God. Everything is bathed in God who is round about us, enveloping us. The fish of your story must let go to find the Is-ness of God. When I preach I often preach of this detachment, letting go of what hinders God in us.

J.P. Is this detachment, or letting go, like a birth effect, that when you let God be born through you, it changes the way you relate to the world and others?

MEISTER Certainly the birth of the Word in you transforms your manner of relating to yourself, the world, others, and God. First, you must let God be born. Just as a woman must accept the presence of one within her when with child and then do all required for labor, so we must first accept the Presence. We must let be what is.

J.P. Detachment is not a popular word in my time. It smacks of a world-denying attitude, a negative view toward creation. It demands sacrifice. This is not a warmly embraced notion in my age, Meister.

MEISTER In comparison to God, all creation is nothing; nothing but what God makes it, the image and spark of Is-ness, energized by the Alivening spirit. We should love all that leads us to God but leave behind all that prevents us from union with God.

J.P. When I was younger and more ignorant than I am, I believed renunciation was a bit neurotic. In my time it has become popular to renounce sacrifice, thereby making religion easy and cheap, for the sake of feeling good. Are you saying then, Meister, that your closeness to God is in proportion to the ascetic practices and sacrifices you demand of yourself?

MEISTER Asceticism is of no great value. There are better ways of living with your passions, feelings, and thoughts than by piling up ascetic practices of self-denial, mortifications, and penances. Outwardly people who insist on their pious practices are holy. Inwardly, however, they may be overly self-conscious and self-centered. They are asses, for they know much about God but do not know God. The task is to break through all that we want to call our own, whether passions, holy practices, or even modes of God, so that Christ the True Word can be born in us. God demands that we be poor in order to be rich in union with love. God asks that we bear all suffering in life as Christ so patiently did, so that Christ may be fruitful in us. We must give God power over all that we are, so that God may transform our suffering into a new birth. We do not seek suffering for its own sake, but that God be born through whatever is in our lives. There is only one reason to pray, to fast, to do good works, or to be baptized. It is the same reason why, most important of all, God became human. The answer is so that God may be born in the soul and the soul be born in God. That is why we have the world, the holy Scriptures, and all God's heavenly natures.

J.P. In my time many people follow a way called the "twelve steps"; they speak often of letting go and letting serenity be. There is also in a school of psychology called psychosynthesis a technique called disidentification, which holds that I am controlled by everything with which I identify myself, and can guide or control everything from which I disidentify. Is the detachment you speak of a disidentification from what you are not, to be born into who you are in God?

MEISTER Yes. I am not God, although the spark is in me. I am not my passions, although I experience God through them. Letting go that God may be God in and through me is the demand of creation. Yet we are so full of ourselves. We have visions, raptures, and desires, thinking these are who we are. We want material gain, power, and notice. There is no room in the inn of our hearts for the indwelling presence of God to be born. We must strip ourselves of this inclination to call everything "mine." If you truly want to have and enjoy the peace of God, you must stand naked of all created things. As long as created things, body, mind, imagination, passions, the world, concepts of God, praying for this or that, peace, and the mineness we cling to, divide us from union with God we will not experience the birth of God through our emptiness. All we can do to bring about the birth of God in us is to rid ourselves of all that is not God in us. God will do the rest.

J.P. Your thought demands a careful listening. What I hear you saying is that we must become so aware of God in all, that we let go of all that is not God.

MEISTER You are correct in your hearing. Be very careful here, however, for I am not saying you must run from pain and pleasure in order to reach some point of mind where you do not care. It is not despairing apathy I counsel, but equanimity and empathy. You used the word "serenity" earlier. Mixed with compassion, it is just what I mean.

You also mentioned "disidentification" when speaking of who or what is the focus of your life. I would use "disengagement," for it calls for renunciation of all that is not God, even of the modes or images we have of God. If a man or woman, for example, clings to drunkenness every day, where is his or her awareness? Or if another clings to a position of power, where is his or her awareness? Is it God they seek, or a false, little god of their own making? God is nothing we can create, for the Godhead is beyond, yet flowing through. We must place all awareness on the True Aliveness of God in all.

J.P. Letting go of everything, even the little happiness I think is mine, in order to find the God to whom I belong, is a frightening request. It is not world-hating, but it demands that I look very hard at what I consider important, what I own in my heart, what I focus my body, passions, and mind on. I would much prefer to pray a little to the God who makes me feel good, or who justifies my ideas and prejudices, or who just lets me alone, than to let go of even these so that Christ may be born through me.

MEISTER Labor is ever difficult, especially the labor of a mother giving birth. What good is it if the eternal birth of the divine Son takes place everywhere, in the virginity of Mary, the world, others, but does not take place in me? What good is it if Mary, who is full of grace, gives birth to the Son of the Creator, if I do not in my heart, in my time, my place? What good is it to give birth to an idea, or image, or prejudice, or attachment if it hinders the true birth of the only Son of God? What good is an image of God if it blinds you to the God who awaits birth in you? If you trust God, God will be born in you. It is, however, only when you let go and let this birth be that you will receive a rich abundance, a new sensitivity, and a wonderful vulnerability. Then in whatever you do or see, observe or hear, in all your relationships with others and with things you will focus on and be taken up in this birth of God. Every person and thing will direct you to God for you have broken through all to God. Then every moment and doing will become for you nothing but God. Keep your eye only on God. Take your grasp from whatever it holds that is not God and you will see it in a new birth of awareness. It is when we let go of all that we break through into the all of the Godhead. It is mind-shattering to strip away our attachments, empty ourselves of ourselves, yet by doing so we discover Christ. There is a someone in our soul awaiting birth. When Christ is born in us, we shall live as we are, children of God.

J.P. Meister, I am almost overwhelmed by what you are saying. I'd love to be able to go on for hours, asking you questions about your teachings and sermons.

MEISTER It has been a long day, and tomorrow I must continue my instruction of the students here at the priory. A regent's job is never done, even when one is being investigated for heresy.

J.P. It is good that you can keep a somewhat humorous outlook. It's almost as though it is all too important to take seriously.

MEISTER The birth of the living Christ is of the greatest importance, beyond all else, but it is God's doing, not mine. My task is to be silent. Every soul in which the birth is to take place must remain very pure, unattached, and must live a life that is collected, noble, and spiritual. The means of birth is silence in a soul where peace and celebration command all attention. When the soul is free and unencumbered, God can generate the Son in the foundation of the soul.

J.P. How silent must our souls be so that God can speak the Son into our lives?

MEISTER We must forget all other noise but the Word of God speaking. We must depart from all creatures and their images in order to be receptive to the secret Word. The more you are without an image, the more open you are to God's influence. God will be effective the more inwardly you are turned and the more forgetful you are of yourself.

J.P. This inner silence without images is almost beyond human comprehension. Most of us seem to need some way of understanding, some form or mode, characteristic, or knowing for God. We are human and therefore must create images to feel and think. Without images of God we sense an absence of God.

MEISTER God is opposed to mere images, for God is beyond them all. We must take leave of all notions and modes of God so that God can be born in the still imageless essence of the soul.

J.P. This is beyond my understanding.

MEISTER Absolutely, but not beyond God's doing. The only image of God to be known and aware of is the Son, the divine Word's birth in us. Let us leave it there. When we speak of divine matters we stammer because we attempt to put into words what we can only experience. That is why silence is best. Let God speak in you so that you can speak God for others. Until God speaks, be silent.

J.P. Is the experience of Christ being born in the human heart something quite extraordinary for only a select few, for only the saints?

MEISTER No. All are called to be the birthplace of the Word, the ground of God. God is not born in the soul of a few ascetics who run away in fear from the reality of the world and things; rather, God becomes incarnate in all those who courageously look deeply within for the sake of compassionate living. We must all learn to penetrate things to find God. If someone, for example, works in a stable, yet experiences a breaking through of God into all creation, a birthing of God, then what should he do? He should return to work in the stable. The mark of a just person is not that of special raptures or position but rather that wherever they are, they hear the word of God and keep it.

J.P. So the effect of this birth of God in us is to thrust us out to work, to do God's work?

MEISTER First, it is to be a child of God. It is a discovery of who you are. Only through a deep self-knowledge do you learn that it is God who is the very ground and foundation of your soul. Our first work is then to know ourselves well enough to know the Christ being born in and through us. Then our work becomes holy. It is not, however, work that makes us holy. It is God who makes holy the works that flow out of our goodness. The work of all is to be compassionate as God is compassion. First be compassionate toward your own body and soul and then toward the bodies and souls of others. As Aristotle reminds us, "Friendship toward others is rooted in being a friend to yourself." In one in whom the Word is born, compassion is born. It is compassion toward self and others that clothes the soul with the robe of God. Our work then is to let compassion be born through our living each ordinary day. Nothing is more holy than such effort.

J.P. What is this compassion that is born through us?

MEISTER It is what I have said, justice. There is a rightness in giving to each person what is his or her due. You show compassion in two ways: in giving and forgiving. When you give others their just due and when you forgive as you have been forgiven, it is compassion at work in you. Compassion is not an impulse out of passion but a deliberate choice and decision to give. Compassion is the highest work that God does in and through all creatures.

J.P. Thomas Merton, a mystic of my time, spoke of compassion as an interdependence between the created world, humanity, and God. Would this word "interdependence" describe the compassionate attitude you speak of?

MEISTER Yes, it would. Whatever may happen to another, whether it be joy or sorrow, happens to me. God has saved the entire world, which should fill us with more joy than if God saved only me or you. You can call God "love" or "goodness," but God's best name is "compassion." If you ask human science to describe or define the soul, it could not for no one knows what the soul actually is. What we do know is that the soul is where God works compassion. God births the word of compassion in our soul and it passes compassion on to our various powers in different ways, as, for example, charity, good intent, or gratitude, or desire. Ultimately, it is God's peace that sustains us and thereby we sustain one another. We enrich one another, Father John, just by being present to one another. God creates all in compassionate interdependence.

J.P. This birthing of compassion is, then, a prayer?

MEISTER Yes, a living, moving prayer of repose. If a person were in ecstatic rapture, however, as marvelous as when St. Paul experienced God, and then learned that a neighbor were in need of soup to eat, it would be better to leave the rapture and help feed that person. The poor cannot be left to God alone. We must each hold firmly in our minds the thought that if compassion is to become, to be realized, it must be through us.

Remember, Father John, God calls all to salvation. So we must become compassion for the whole world. We must bid that this very earth become a heaven. We must keep running, running, running for peace. Let us pray especially to be freed from a sense of greediness for there is no such thing as my bread, my land, my clothing. All things for life are on loan to us. All bread and all earth are ours, not mine.

J.P. As we talk about this birth of compassion in the world, I can't help but recall something I have heard while traveling recently in the Rhine area. I've been told that in some churches there is placed a baby's crib so that women wishing to become mothers can go to church to rock the crib in expectation. This crib image is what comes to me as we speak of letting go so that God may be born in us and the world so that ultimately we may all be born back to God.

MEISTER That is an old Bavarian custom and quite beautiful. What else does God do all day long but give birth. And we are meant to be the spiritual mothers of God, rocking until peace is born. Did not Mary the Mother prepare for the birth of the Son of God? In every moment God needs to be born. We must be the mothers of this God.

J.P. Meister, our time grows short, so before I go let me thank you for seeing me. May I say, no matter what happens at the proceedings against the orthodoxy of some of your teachings, your sermons and books will have many new births in the years ahead. In fact, in my time your message is waking up many men and women to a much more simple, ordinary, earthly, and healthy faith.

MEISTER Thank you.

Meister Eckhart of Hochheim died shortly before April 30, 1328, after having been called to Avignon, France, where an official papal commission of theologians was appointed to review the Meister's case and examine the articles suspected of heretical or false teaching. Almost one year after the Meister's death Pope John XXII issued a bull In argro dominico, in which 26 articles from Eckhart's Latin works were listed, of which the first 15 were declared heretical and the remaining 11 termed "dangerous and suspect of heresy." A further two articles from German sermons were condemned. The bull ended with the statement that Eckhart had before his death revoked and denounced all such statements of his that were declared heretical or dangerous.

According to a growing consensus of noted and reputable Catholic scholars, Meister Eckhart was surely innocent of heresy regarding 15 articles taken out of context from his writings and sermons. Some suggest that Eckhart's difficulties lay in being too imaginative in an age when theological creativity was strongly suspect. Eckhart was a theological artist, not a bureaucrat. In May 1983, the Master General of the Dominicans instituted the Eckhart Commission, which in 1986 recommended an official declaration be made by the pope acknowledging the exemplary character of Meister Eckhart's preaching, stating also that his writings and sermons are an authentic expression of Christian mysticism, and therefore trustworthy guides to Christian life according to the spirit of the gospel. On October 28, 1985, in a discourse before a distinguished audience Pope John Paul II quoted Meister Eckhart: "Did not Eckhart teach his disciples: All that God asks you most pressingly is to go out of yourself. . . and let God be God in you?"

Suggested Readings

Meister Eckhart: The Essential Sermons, Commentaries, Treatises, and Defense (The Classics of Western Spirituality Series), trans. and introd. Edmund Colledge, O.S.A. and Bernard McGinn. Mahwah, N.J.: Paulist Press, 1981.

Eckhart's Way: The Way of the Christian Mystics, vol. 2, by Richard Woods, O.P. Wilmington, Del.: Michael Glazier, Inc., 1986.

Meister Eckhart: Sermons & Treatises, vol. 1, trans. & ed. M. O'Connell Walshe. Somerset, England: Watkins Pub., 1979.

Breakthrough: Meister Eckhart's Creation Spirituality in New Translation, introduction & commentary by Matthew Fox, O.P. New York: Doubleday, 1980.

Meditations with Meister Eckhart: A Centering Book, by Matthew Fox, O.P. Santa Fe, N.M.: Bear & Co., 1983.

The Man From Whom God Hid Nothing: Meister Eckhart, ed. Ursula Fleming. London: Fount Paperbacks, 1988.

Meister Eckhart: Thought & Language by Frank Tobin. Philadelphia: University of Pennsylvania Press, 1986.

The Way of Paradox, by Cyprian Smith. Mahwah, N.J.: Paulist Press, 1987.

Excerpts from the readings of MEISTER ECKHART OF HOCHHEIM

"One also finds many names for God in the Bible. Yet despite all of this I maintain that whenever someone recognizes something in God and puts a name on it, then it is not God. God is higher than names or nature."

Essential Sermons, Sermon 1

"It is good that a person has a peaceful life; it is better that a person bear a troublesome life with patience. But best of all is that a person can have peace even in the very midst of trouble."

Essential Sermons, Sermon 9

"The one who knows God best is the one who recognizes him equally everywhere."

Essential Sermons, Sermon 9

"God has acted exactly like people who hide themselves and then clear their throats, thus giving themselves away. No one could ever have discovered God, but he has now given himself away."

Essential Sermons, Sermon 10

"This is why Saint Augustine says that the most beautiful thing which a person can say about God consists in that person's being silent from the wisdom of an inner wealth. So be silent and do not flap your gums about God, for the extent that you flap your gums about God, you lie and you commit sin."

Essential Sermons, Sermon 11

"Now God longs for nothing from you more than that you should emerge from yourself in accord with your being as a creature, and that you should admit God within yourself."

Essential Sermons, Sermon 14

"People must be so empty of all things and all works, whether inward or outward, that they can become a proper home for God, wherein God may operate."

Essential Sermons, Sermon 15

"Many people plead with God for everything that he can do for them. They do not wish, however, to give God all they are capable of giving."

Essential Sermons, Sermon 16

"Wait only for this birth within yourself, and you will discover all blessing and all consolation, all bliss, all being and all truth."

Essential Sermons, Sermon 18

"Our happiness, however, does not lie in our accomplishments but rather in the fact that we undergo God."

Essential Sermons, Sermon 18

"Thus the Father generates His Son in the true unity of the divine nature. Behold, in the same and no other way God the father generates his Son in the foundation of the soul and in its being, and he thus unites himself with the soul."

Essential Sermons, Sermon 21

"The Father's speaking is his giving birth; the Son's listening is his being born."

Essential Sermons, Sermon 22

"Where my soul is, there is God, and where God is, there my soul is also."

Essential Sermons, Sermon 28

"Or according to Aristotle, 'Friendship toward others is rooted in the ability to be a friend to oneself.' How then can anyone be compassionate toward me or toward you who is not compassionate toward himself?"

Essential Sermons, Sermon 28

Jan Van Ruysbroeck
(1293 - 1381)

My interview with Prior Jan Van Ruysbroeck, formerly a parish priest for 26 years at St. Gudule's Parish in the heart of the Flemish city of Brussels, took place in Groenendael, in a solitary green valley some 10 kilometers outside the city. The interview with Prior Ruysbroeck, now retired but an active spiritual guide for his community of Canons Regular of Saint Augustine, was arranged by a friend and spiritual son, Gerard Grott, the eventual founder of the Brothers of the Common Life.

Master Grott had informed me that Prior Ruysbroeck would meet me at the front of the priory at 4:00 P.M. at which time I could join the prior for his daily walk. It seemed Prior Ruysbroeck enjoyed sitting under a specific tree in the quiet of the forest, and at age 71 he needed some assistance in walking. Since I was interviewing him I could replace the brother who would be sent along to assist the prior. The date was April 15, 1364. I was anxious to meet this holy, remarkable man, now often called "Ruysbroeck the Admirable," for he had a reputation of being a quiet and warm man, yet one who fought vehemently against what he believed to be the false teachings of his day. I had read almost all the prior's major writings: *The Kingdom of the Lovers of God, The Spiritual Espousals, The Sparkling Stone,* and *The Mirror of Eternal Salvation,* but had not yet seen some of his most recent smaller works, especially *The Little Book of Clarifications.* As I stood outside the small doors of the priory, behind which solitude reigned supreme, I could not help but wonder why a priest, after over 25 years of parish work, would move out into a forest so thick and isolated. At ten past four, my mind wandered into my own need for greater inner and outer quiet and how difficult it was to be still even when I stole the time away for prayerful meditation. Perhaps the matter of how the prior reaches the supreme summit and integration of going in (rest) and going out (work) at once would be a good starting point for our discussion. We would see.

It was 4:20 when the door behind was jarred open to let the small figure of Prior Ruysbroeck out. The large brother who had obviously shoved the door open, handed over the Prior's shoulder a tablet and stylus, informing me gently that I might be asked to take notes if the prior wished to do some writing. As I took the instruments from the brother's hand, I could not help but notice that the prior's religious habit was a bit of a mess, with at least two noticeable holes in one sleeve. When I instinctively took the prior's arm in greeting, I knew I was in the presence of a "seer" who found living in the world of appearance a bit difficult. As we walked across the garden toward the forest, the prior spoke first.

PRIOR I am sorry for my tardiness. I was delayed by a cleric of the city who considers himself quite important. He arrived unannounced wishing to talk with me at length about his spiritual life and to complain, it seems, about the lack of support from the people of his parish. He thinks they should be taxed further for his care, as if they are not already taxed enough by the church, and as if he needs more care than he already takes for himself. A bit of a fool, poor man. Sadly, the people pay for such arrogance.

J.P. If you would prefer to do this interview a bit later, Prior, it would give you a chance to talk with him.

PRIOR No, no. I must confess I am getting rather blunt in my later years. I have already told him what he needs and, although he did not know it, wanted to hear. I told him, you are as holy as you wish to be. I recommended he put aside the ways of arrogance, thinking the people should support his rather high style of living. I felt if I were stern, ignoring his self-importance, he might grow angry enough to pray to the Lord for guidance. It is bad enough that we have men and women of free spirit who believe they are exempt from human life, thinking themselves to be God, doing as they please in body while certain they have reached perfection. While these so-called free of spirit romp around inflicting harm on the people, the church and pompous clerics seek more taxes from a people already supporting wars, crusades, and scandalous habits among some clergy and religious who have forgotten their vows of poverty. I know that no one truly understands what love is, but this I know; it gives more than you can take and asks more than you can give. I have sent this self-righteous cleric on his way with a thoughtful story in hopes that it will open the eyes of his soul to see that the bridegroom, the Lord, is coming. He had better go out to meet him, or he will be left outside to freeze in his own coldness of heart.

J.P. What story did you tell him that might open his eyes, that he might become a God-seeing man?

PRIOR I told him a simple story that Meister Eckhart often told. I repeat it frequently to the spiritually immature. We are all young once, but we can remain spiritually immature all our lives. The story is about a learned man, like the cleric who just left the priory in a huff. The learned man of our story searched for many years for a teacher to give him the truth. Once, when he felt a great emptiness within his heart, he heard the voice of God, which speaks without utterance and without the sound of words, say, "Go to the church, and there you will find a man who shall show you the way to union with God." Off the learned man went only to find a poor man whose feet were torn, was covered with dust and dirt, and whose clothes were little more than rags. The educated gentleman greeted the poor man:

"I hope you have a good day!"

The poor man answered, "I have never had a bad day!"

"God gives you good luck then," said the learned man.

"I have never had bad luck," said the beggar.

Frustrated at the poor man's answers the learned man said, "Well, may you be happy!"

Quietly and without fluster the poor man answered, "I have never been unhappy."

"How can this be," exclaimed the learned fellow. "Please, explain it to me," he asked the poor man. The beggar fellow answered willingly, "You wished me to have a good day. I have never really had a bad day, for if I am hungry, I praise God. If it freezes, hails, rains, if the weather is fair or stormy, I praise God. If I am despised and looked down upon, I praise God, and so I never have an evil day. You wished that God would send me a bit of luck. But I never had bad luck, for I know how to live with God. I know what God has done is best for me, for what God ordains for me, whether good or ill by my estimate, I take cheerfully as the best that can be, so I have never had bad luck. You wished that God would make me happy. I was never unhappy, for I only desire to live in the will of God. What God wills, I will."

"But," asked the learned man, "what if God willed to throw you into hell? What would you do then? Answer that!"

"Throw me into hell?" said the poor man in surprise. "God's goodness forbids such. But if God did throw me into hell, I would embrace this God with both arms. My left arm would be a humble attitude that would unite me to God's humanity in Christ and the right arm would embrace with love, which would unite me to God's divinity. I would embrace God with humility and love so that God would have to go with me to hell. I would rather be in hell with God, than in heaven without."

The learned man then realized that humble abandonment is the surest way to God. He then asked the poor man, "Where are you from?"

"From God."

"Where did you find God?"

"When I looked within, yet beyond, all creatures."

"Where have you left God then?" asked the gentleman.

"In the pure hearts of people filled with good will," he answered.

The learned fellow gently asked, "What sort of man are you?"

"I am a king," was the answer, "and my soul is my kingdom, for I can so rule my senses inward and outward that all the desires of body and power of soul are subjected to God. This kingdom is greater than any kingdom on earth."

"How did you achieve such a summit?" the learned man asked with a new understanding of how poorly ignorant he was.

"Through silence, good thoughts and through union with God," answered the poor fellow. "I could never rest in anything that is less than God. Now, however, I have found God and have eternal peace."

Isn't that a story to open anyone's eyes, Father John?

J.P. It is, Prior, but you said you told the cleric a simple story. This story you tell is about humility, abandonment, contemplation, love and union with God. It is simply complex.

PRIOR No, it's not. It is simple because it will draw all to God. God draws us out, God draws us in, God draws us to rest in the super-essential life of unity.

J.P. Prior, could you pass that one by me one more time at a little slower pace?

PRIOR The divine persons who form one sole God are in their nature ever active, and in the simplicity of their essence form the Godhead and eternal blessedness. God, considering each Person, is eternal work, but the essence of God is eternal rest. What God says to each human soul is, "You are mine and I am yours; I am yours and you are mine, for I have chosen you from all eternity."

J.P. When you say, Prior, that God is activity, are you saying God is the shining, the burning, the flowing, the birthing, the speaking?

PRIOR Yes.

J.P. And when you say God is eternal rest do you mean God is also the light, the fire, the river, the mother, the speaker, and the word spoken?

PRIOR Yes, and what are we, young priest, in our deepest soul, in what makes us like God?

J.P. A beam, a spark, a moist form, a child, a byword.

PRIOR Yes, that is God in eternal activity and eternal rest. You forgot something, however, John. God is also courting and spousing nature and creation into union. God is courting with love that we might be drawn to the groom who is God at rest.

J.P. So God goes out in activity and draws all into rest.

PRIOR Yes, Father John. But do not be distracted by the many and thereby miss the one love of God that continually swings between and reconciles two questions: "What is God?" and "What am I?" God's love is unifying love in motion, an outgoing attraction that drags us out of ourselves, calling us to be melted into unity. Each of us has an inherent impulse to be drawn by God. Like a child striving toward adulthood, we strive to grow in unity with God through love, detachment, and education.

J.P. So what you are saying is that as God is eternal activity and eternal rest, we are called to live in this same harmony?

PRIOR Let me speak again as simply as I can. A person goes toward God with loving activity and works, enters into God with an inclination toward eternal rest and contemplation, therefore remaining in God, yet nevertheless goes out to all creatures in a common love for all. This is what I like to call the storm of love, when two spirits struggle: the Spirit of God and our spirit. God inclines toward us through the activity of the Holy Spirit. We are thereby touched with love. Our spirit or self or soul, by means of God's activity and loving powers, is impelled, driven toward God. Thereby God is touched by us who are impelled. This is the simple synthesis of love.

J.P. Do you possibly have a story that might in some way illustrate how we might experience this loving union with God?

PRIOR Well, it is an inadequate story at best, but for those living in the storm of love, for endurance sake, I will tell you a parable about an ant. Now the ant is small but mighty. It carries its weight many times over. It lives in a community by choice whether in hot or dry soil. During the summer the ant works to prepare for winter, gathering and splitting grain so that the community will have enough for the cold. All the ants follow a single path. No ant follows strange paths. If it waits until its proper time, the ant will be able to fly.

J.P. Are you saying, Prior, that we should act like the ants?

PRIOR Yes. We should be strong in waiting for Christ the Lord to come and resilient in warding off and avoiding the temptation to follow a strange and singular path. We should live in the unity of our heart as the ant in the community of ants, with each power, emotion, desire, memory, intellect, imagination, following the invitation to oneness with God. In the hot and dry country, God will be at home if we work for the summer gathering the grain of good works and virtues to be ready for the cold times. The only way to God is the way of love, the imprinted impulse in our souls. If we await this appropriate time and persevere in good works, then we will see the mystery of God and fly toward it.

J.P. The ant becomes what it must become. We, however, have a choice of seeing or not seeing God. It is our choice.

PRIOR It is not just choice, however, Father. There are three things necessary for seeing the one Lord, or Bridegroom, out of the many enticing grooms or loves in life. First, the light of God's grace or affirming presence; second, a will that is freely turned toward God; and lastly, a conscience free from sin. In other words, you need the light of the sun, a willingness to look at the object, and eyes that are healthy and capable of focus. The light of grace is given to all if they but turn their soul from other loves to the one true groom of God, focusing their attention on the one who comes to meet them.

J.P. Where do you see this God-groom coming?

Prior First, God reveals blessedness and richness to us in the created world. We can savor God there. The second coming of Christ, the Bridegroom, takes place every day in good persons who use their gifts and abilities wisely. The third coming of Christ is in the future when we experience death and are transformed in judgment. Christ goes out of God as an ideal model saying to your spirit and soul, "Go out" to God.

J.P. Our call, then, is to go out to Christ?

PRIOR Yes. The Bridegroom is coming, we must go out to meet him. How do we do this, you may ask? Well, we do it in three ways; by going out to God, to ourselves, and to our neighbor.

J.P. I see.

PRIOR Whom do you see?

J.P. No, I understand a bit more now...your talking of love. No wonder it is confusing, almost maddening. Human love is often felt to drive people mad. Divine Love certainly motivates holy madness.

PRIOR Few of us are called to the divine, super-essential vision, either because we are not fit or because we don't stand in the light. No one shall completely understand this vision of unity with God by means of study and research. For all human words, learning and understanding falls short of touching this truth. Words can never imprison the Divine Lover.

J.P. The title of what many consider your greatest work is *Spiritual Espousals*. What does this book say of love?

PRIOR Christ is the Bridegroom of nature, uniting our nature with him in love. He labors as our champion against our foes, freeing us from prison and winning the battle. Through death we have life. Through blood we have been ransomed and through the water of baptism we have been set free. We are enriched and clad with the gifts of Christ's love.

J.P. I must say this Bridegroom Christ sounds like a warrior or knight going to battle for the fair maiden, what you describe as the soul of our nature.

PRIOR Love is God's selfhood. It is not merely a passionate sentiment but a holy energy, a mighty force that fills the universe. Loving is the essential activity of God. Like lightning between God and the soul, God is loving in a raging fire, a storm, a flood, a forever of giving and taking. God is pouring energy into the soul and drawing out of the soul new life, surrender, and generous love. Our entire life and way of growth depends entirely on our courage of heart, industry of body, and will to accept our part in this divine give and take, push and pull. Like a burning love that is immeasurable, love is God in the depths of our spirit. God's love is so ravenous that it swallows and consumes, in its own being, everything that comes near it. God's love is that of a raging bridegroom in search of his spouse.

J.P. Prior, I want to ask about...

PRIOR Excuse me, Father, let me correct one point. I did not title any of my works. Others have done that.

J.P. I'm sorry, Prior, I did not know. I wanted to ask again about this love meeting between God and nature, or God and our essential self.

PRIOR Well, as you know, every encounter or meeting in relationships is between two persons coming together from different directions and places. In the relationship between God and ourselves Christ comes from above as a generous benefactor and an almighty Lord, while we come from below as poor servants who are in deep need. We carry nothing to this encounter. Christ comes to us from within, outward, while we come to Christ from without, inward. What rises, then, is a spiritual meeting.

J.P. Although God and nature come from different places and are in a sense separate, God, nature, our spirit, and Christ, forever possess one another in some fashion.

PRIOR Yes. The human spirit or soul possesses God in its empty and naked nature, and God possesses the human spirit, for it lives in God and God in it. You see, Father, God is the living pattern of creation who in love has impressed the image of that pattern on each human soul and spirit. In every adult spirit the character of that image must be drawn or brought out of hiding to be realized in a living love common to all. There is in you and me, and every person, divine likeness, a spark of the primal fire, a sparkling stone upon which is written a new name. Under the energy and stimulus of God's love, which beats in and on us constantly from within and without, we can grow into the super-essential life. If we feed on the love of Christ, there is a renewing; a rebirthing to a higher yet simpler level of contact with reality. In such a super-essential synthesis we become deiform, in God's image, ever at work for God and ever at rest in God.

Every part of ourselves, intellect, memory, will, body, and in whatever we love, is invaded and enhanced by the living pattern of creation. It is our naked, emptied, and essential spirits that relate most fully and simply with God, for we are hidden children and friends of God. We must grow into such children, such hidden friends. Never do we become God, but rather God inhabits our home as we become who we are. It is the Divine Light that penetrates the surrendered, drenches the naked soul, and fills the empty country of our spirits as sunshine penetrates, drenches, and fills the earth and air as fire does the iron. The air does not become the sun nor the iron the fire, but can air live on in fruitfulness without the sun or the iron be bent without the fire? We are God-formed because God overflows. See, the Lord is coming. Go out to meet him.

J.P. Before we began this discussion or interview, Prior, I thought to ask you first about the concept you speak of concerning the eternal activity and rest of God, a going out and drawing back as it applies practically to each of us. I am a young priest and searcher for God, perhaps a bit like yourself when you worked in a parish as curate some years ago. I am not sure, but perhaps like you once did, I now struggle with the issues of work and rest or activity and silence. The time is short and. . .

PRIOR Now, John. Do not presume to think that I am fully and always living in the country of God's super-essential life or am so simple as to have eternally reconciled the activity and stillness of God within me. For 26 years, John, I worked as a curate in a parish in one of the busiest of cities. It is true that I often felt frustrated in having to steal time from activity for interior contemplation. My life was so taken up with work and there was so much scandal and hostility around our church that my companions and I chose to move to this forest. We desired an atmosphere of solitude and silence so that we could focus our eyes and ears on the eternal coming of God within our spirits, or the eternal marriage of God and nature.

After many years in this forest priory I must say that we are still taken up with much activity in service of the many who come to us for guidance. The life of the righteous person, one living in super-essential union with God, is always in flux, reflux, and eternal rest. In stillness, love moves and in eternal activity, love rests. When and wherever you experience God, John, when and wherever you see the Lord coming, you must let your natural impulse lead you out to meet him. Then you will experience the simple synthesis of activity and rest. They will no longer be in opposition but integrated as you are in union with God.

If you give yourself, John, only to external activity or only to interior idleness and passivity, you will not understand what I have said concerning union with God. My hidden friend of God, turn your body, your reason, and your will, with all their potency to the spirits gazing, to faith, to what is above body, reason, and will. Turn your senses to the spirit in you and God will overflow, immersing your spirit and senses in super-essential unity, where union without distinction is found.

J.P. Prior, I thank you for the walk and for our conversation. I'm sorry we never stopped to rest under your favorite tree.

PRIOR Oh, John, but we did. If you are willing to walk with God along the lofty ways of love, you will rest with God without end. John, God beholds the dwelling place, the home he has made with you and in you. That dwelling place of spirit is your unity and likeness to God. God wants to visit your inner land of unity as a bridegroom or as a new birthplace for Christ. Let the Lord come and walk with you in your essential spirit, the dwelling place you are, John.

J.P. In this age of great excess of arrogance, wealth, and poverty you stand out as quite an uncommon man, Prior.

PRIOR No, John, I am only trying to live the common life. Before you leave, John, would you like to share in the jewel that Christ has given us for the sake of unity; the supper of the high feast where Christ's humanity feeds our humanity, overflows into our bodily natures, adorns and illuminates our spirits? In the sacrament of the altar, we are given the exalted personality of the one who comes. Together we can go out to meet the Lord in the Bread of Life. Through this sacrament, let us be united and drawn back to the Father. Thus we shall come into our inheritance, the divinity in everlasting blessing. In the sacrament our natures can do little else but take on the delight of Christ's humanity, glory, joys, and honors.

J.P. I would be happy to join you for the Lord's sacrament.

On December 2, 1381, Jan Van Ruysbroeck died at the age of 88, at the Monastery of Groenendael, where he was also buried. In 1783, however, his remains were returned to St. Gudule's, the parish in which he had served as curate. In 1909, Jan Van Ruysbroech was declared blessed by the Catholic church.

Suggested Readings

John Ruysbroeck: The Spiritual Espousals and Other Works, introd. and transl. James A. Wiseman, O.S.B. (The Classics of Western Spirituality). Mahwah, N.J.: Paulist Press, 1985.

Ruysbroeck, The Admirable, by A. Wautier D'Aygalliers. Kennikat Press, Inc. Distributed in the United States by Christian Classics, Westminster, Md., 1969.

Blessed Jan Van Ruysbroeck: The Spiritual Espousals, transl. from Dutch with introd. by Eric Colledge. Christian Classics, Westminster, Md., 1983.

Ruysbroeck, by Evelyn Underhill. London: G. Bell and Sons Ltd., London, 1915.

Excerpts from the writings of JAN VAN RUYSBROECK

"See, the bridegroom is coming. Go out to meet him."
The Spiritual Espousals, Part One

"Christ, the wisdom of the Father, has from the time of Adam spoken to all persons in an interior manner according to his divinity, addressing them with the word 'see.'"
The Spiritual Espousals, Part One

"There are three things that are required [to see]: the light of God's grace, a will that is freely turned toward God, and a conscience free of mortal sin."
The Spiritual Espousals, Part One

"For this reason we shall have to consider three comings of our Bridegroom Jesus Christ. In the first of these comings he became a human being out of love for us. The second coming takes place daily in many and various ways in every longing heart, for he comes with new gifts and new graces according to the measure in which each person is able to receive them. The third coming is that on the Day of Judgement or at the hour of death."
The Spiritual Espousals, Part Two

"This going out is to be done in three ways: We must go out to God and to ourselves and to our neighbor, and this must be done with charity and righteousness. Charity constantly strives upward toward the kingdom of God, that is, to God himself, for he is the source from which charity has flowed forth without intermediary and in which it abides by means of union."
The Spiritual Espousals, Part Three

"When a person through the grace of God is able to see and has a purified conscience, and when he has observe the three comings of Christ our Bridegroom, and when he has gone out in virtuous activity, there then follows a meeting with our Bridegroom, which is the fourth and last point. In this meeting lies our entire salvation."

The Spiritual Espousals, Part Four

"The Spirit of God therefore says in St. John's Book of Revelation: 'to the one who overcomes'—that is, to the one who overcomes and transcends himself and all things—'I will give the hidden bread of heaven'—that is, an interior, hidden and heavenly joy—and I will give him a sparkling stone. On this stone a new name will be written, unknown to everyone except him who receives it."

The Sparkling Stone

"Whoever feels himself to be united with God savors this name in accordance with the degree of his virtue, of his ascent to God, and of his unity with him. In order that everyone might receive his name and possess it forever, the Lamb of God—that is, our Lord's humanity—delivered himself up to death and opened for us the Book of Life, in which the names of all the elect stand written. No one of these names can be blotted out, for they are one with that living book which is the Son of God. That same death broke open for us the seals of this book, so that all virtues might come to fulfillment in accordance with God's eternal providence."

The Sparkling Stone

Johannes Tauler
(c. 1300 - 1361)

Rulman Merswin, a well-to-do merchant of Strasbourg, had warned me of the dangers when he wrote in reply to my request for an interview with Brother Johannes Tauler, the famous Dominican preacher of preachers from Strasbourg, a man known in almost every convent, monastery, and village in the Rhine and low countries of Germany. Mr. Merswin had warned me to avoid, if at all possible, the city limits of Strasbourg and to move quickly to his home outside the city where a gathering of the "Friends of God" was to take place on this bitterly frigid night of February 1349. An invitation had been extended to me to join this gathering of clerics, nuns, men, and women for prayers and devotion, and to then enjoy a talk by Brother Tauler on the three births of God. After the meeting I was told I could interview the speaker if convenient.

With these fairly stable plans I traveled as quickly as I could to join the friends, only to run headlong into obstacles that taught me again to be flexible and patient. On the road before me, just outside the city of Strasbourg, I was stuck behind a snaking procession of hundreds of men dressed in black hooded robes, being led by a man bearing a cross as they chanted and moaned, "Spare us, oh God." Hundreds of women and children as well followed this frightening march of what I had been warned might be flagellants, doing penance for the sins they believed had caused what is known as the greatest biological event in history, the bubonic and pneumonic epidemic, or plague: the Black Death. The flagellants moved slowly, gathering members as they headed for the city square to beat themselves with spike-tipped whips for the remission of sin. As I slowly followed this march of death, looking for a side road that might free me from this obstruction, I could not help but think of the Shiites in Iran, beating themselves in holy obedience in the hope that they would win a war, or the religious men and women who symbolically hit themselves with ropes of discipline to remind themselves how unworthy they were to be embraced in God's love. I knew from history that the Black Death had wiped out perhaps 25 to 50 percent of Europe; that Pope Clement VI had estimated the death toll at the unbelievable number of 23,840,000 people; that monasteries, convents, and villages were devastated, but I could not help but think also of the people of my own time who suffered the plagues of famine in Ethiopia, oppression in South Africa, holocaust in Europe, open grave burial in Haiti, AIDS in the United States. It seems every age has its devastation as well as flagellants who blame social and biological ills on the evil human heart.

Arriving finally at the home of Rulman Merswin, I was informed that the group of Friends had not met that night because of a disastrous occurrence in the city that day. It seems the new town council of Strasbourg had actually carried out its threat to burn the city's 2000 Jews, believing that the plague was due to the Jews poisoning the wells. Rumor also had it that in the city of Basel the Jews had been rounded up, put on an island in the Rhine, and burned. The Friends had decided that they would go into the city to protest to council members the burning of Jews that Pope Clement VI had specifically denounced.

Brother Tauler, however, had remained behind to wait for my arrival. He would proceed to the city after our discussion to meet with those council members he could before nightfall and then minister at a local convent set up as a clinic for those dying from the plague. I was shaken by what I had seen in the city and stunned by what I heard, imagining then the millions of Jews who would in the future of six hundred years be gassed and put in the ovens. I sat down to interview the preacher without the slightest idea of what to ask. My question merely fell out of my lips without plan or direction.

J.P. I understand, Brother Tauler, that you had gathered tonight with your friends and God's friends to speak on the three births of God. Is that correct?

BROTHER Yes, Father John. Although it is February, with Christmas and Ephiphany past and with the Easter feast rapidly approaching, I was tonight going to share some thoughts on how God enters our soul as in a birth. Actually, on Christmas we celebrate three Christmas Masses to recall the three births of God; the eternal begetting of the Son and Word by God the Father; the very birth of Jesus himself from the womb of Mary the Virgin; and lastly, the birth of God taking place at every hour on every day by grace being born in the souls of good men and women. This ongoing birth of God in the soul takes place out of God's love for us if we but clear the inner ground for this blessed event. God does not seem able or willing to stop himself from birthing the Word in our souls if we willingly respond to his love by purifying and purging ourselves of alien gods; greed, the inordinate pleasure we take in things, judgmental attitudes, laziness, anger, and violence. If the birth of God is to take place within, one must dispose the inner ground by turning away from all that is not purely God. For God to enter the soul, we must make way by abandoning what is not God; images, worldly notions, external possessions. This does not mean, of course, that you cannot own a kingdom or work for goods, but only that you must be cold to things, detached from them as transitory and temporary so that only God is warm in the dwelling of your soul. What must claim our attention, awareness, and heart is God alone. All else we need and do, even work, must be dependent upon the God born within the inner person. God is everything good. To the degree that God made all, all is good. We cannot, however, center on worldly goods; rather, we must become oblivious to them in order to be taken over by God's birth in us. Do we not all thirst for God in the deepest recesses of our hearts? Does not humanity desire most a return to the source of its ground? Tonight, here in this home of the Friends of God, I was going to speak of the detachment necessary to be totally immersed in God. I was going to pray that God would help us prepare a dwelling place for this most noble birth, so that all of us may become spiritual mothers. If in an entire year you accomplished nothing more than a fleeting glimpse of your soul, it would be a year well spent, a year for celebration and jubilation. For then you would know in awe the place of Christ's birth in you.

J.P. Brother, I find it rather interesting that on the night when it seems thousands of Jews have been murdered out of ignorant fear, while many other people die of plague and are carried out of town heaped on carts to be buried, you speak with such wonder and hope about the birth of Christ in the ground of the soul. I am not criticizing here but rather reacting, I suppose, to the day and events. In my time there are some people so filled with enthusiastic exuberance and positive spiritual ideas that they seem at times to naively bounce over reality, especially painful realities.

BROTHER Father John, this city is my home. I was born here some 49 years ago. I grew up here and was educated in this city. Except for a short period of studies and some years in

Basel when Strasbourg was under papal interdict, I have lived and preached here. I know and love these people. I have spent hours preaching to and teaching many of those who are now dead from the epidemic. I have sat in the homes and by the side of my brothers and sisters in religion who have been dying. I have cried for the people I love in my own community of St. Dominic who have ministered to and consoled the poor. If that were not enough pain, I have then humbly had to preach at their funeral Masses. I have preached against the violence of the flagellants and the cruelty of the roving bands of Jews, I have cared for the sick and preached for the dying. What would you have me do, Father John? Join the flagellants who have despaired into complaint against God, tempted by the hounds that chase them into self-righteousness? How should I respond to the deaths I have seen, to the suffering I feel for those I love?

J.P. I was not questioning the depth of your experience of joy or pain Brother. The way you handle present realities seems to give you peace amid the torments and compassion amid the joys. It is obvious how God has touched you.

BROTHER "Grasped" is a better word, Father John; "touched" is far too clean. How you deal with suffering tells whether you are a true friend of God's or a false friend. The false friends refer everything that happens in their lives to themselves. When afflicted with pain or sorrow, they do not know which way to turn. They tend to run in circles, round and round, looking for advice and comfort. When they do not find escape, what happens but a breakdown into despair? If you have not found God within your inmost ground, there is no foundation upon which to build the house of hope. If the cornerstone of that inner house is not Christ, then what can hold you back from crumbling when pain attacks? The question to ask when suffering is whose friend will you be: God's and therefore truly your own, or your own and therefore falsely God's?

J.P. Brother, there is a theologian of my time (whom many would also describe as a mystic) by the name of Karl Rahner, who may have a point to make here. I have only recently read what he wrote in a journal about suffering. Let me quote it: "We live in an age in which the question is not so much how as sinners we must gain access to a gracious God who will justify us; on the contrary the impression is that it is God. . . who must justify himself to his creatures in their distress while they for their part have no need of justification." [6]

BROTHER Excellent, Father. In my age that is also the question, whether we will be God's true friends, taking refuge in God when in pain and suffering, or whether we will be so self-absorbed that we refuse to turn everything back to God, gifts or adversities. A true friend returns all that has been given to the giver and source, thus opening a free-flowing passage upon which God can come to us and we can travel to God. It is so very sad to see those who have become so self-conscious in their suffering that they become frozen of heart. True friends love themselves in God, not in the multiplicity of themselves and things of their own making.

J.P. But, Brother, we all tend at times, even with the best intentions, to create for ourselves a bit of hell, to take the wrong road. If I remember correctly, the psychologist William James will say in 600 years something like "the hell to be endured hereafter, of which theology tells, is no worse than the hell we make for ourselves in this world by habitually fashioning our characters in the wrong way." [7]

BROTHER That sounds like something Brother Thomas Aquinas would have said. However, he probably would have put it, "It is better to hobble along the right road than run along the wrong!" No matter who we are, Father John, we must be extraordinarily conscious of the hounds that chase and tempt us along the way. Certainly we can all be tempted to great evil, but for most it is the little temptations that can be the most dangerous and difficult to deal with, especially for those whose hearts thirst for union with God. It is the petty flaws we hardly pay attention to, the superficial concerns that bite at our heels and become preoccupations and obsessions, frivolous occupations such as the vanity of fine clothes, having friends who are deemed important or even thoughtlessly innocent recreations that cause our hearts to be mauled by the little terriers of temptation. Once the heart, however, is worn out and thirsty, the huntsmen often holds the hounds and terriers back a bit for another day of chasing.

J.P. Your description of temptation as a chasing dog that snaps at the feet as one travels life's path is one I believe many in my time can relate to. In fact, I am thinking now of the number of people addicted to various substances or abusive processes of emotion or relationship that would describe their struggle with their particular temptation as "getting the monkey off their backs." Anyone attempting to break the chain of destructive habits, confronting the temptations that would destroy their hearts, knows that it is only a change of attitude about who they are that will ultimately save them.

BROTHER Perhaps we must try every path until there is no other path open to us but God, in whom rests all consolation, all truth, and all peace. If you truly wish to overcome temptation, however, but find you cannot outrun the hounds, then you must run as fast as you can to the tree of Christ's cross and passion. There you can crush the head of any thing, feeling, need, or desire that may have control of and tear at your heart. By looking on the cross you can go beyond yourself, falling into God's arms, yet rising up again. Look how Christ suffered the greatest of torments and temptations to despair, yet what did Christ do but submit to God's love. We too must submit to God by living with whatever we suffer in life as ours to deal with, carry, and rise through. What truly remains of a person formed in the image of God, but a soul full of God and a body full of suffering. I do not mean this in any morbid way; it is rather the way of living. If we, however, allow God to take over and build our character, he will build in us a heavenly heart, and even though we live, we carry heaven within us. If we suffer in mind or body and meet Christ in the heaven of our hearts, what peaceful words do you think he will say? Will he not say, "I am pleased with you because you have helped me carry my cross"? In that heaven there is joy and peace.

J.P. You just reminded me of another very famous psychologist of the future who will say something like, and this is not an exact quote, "In every human being, there is a special heaven, whole and unbroken."

BROTHER I am not sure this psychologist you mention

is the first to say such, but he is correct. If we desire to enter this heavenly heart, we must keep careful watch over ourselves. We must remain aware of the ground of our souls, the source from which we flow. We must be learners who are humble enough to know our place before God, dominated always by the one God rather than the many alien gods of our making. A good person is truly a heaven to God. Perhaps this physician friend of yours had an opportunity to read one of my sermons. I understand that some of the nuns to whom I have preached have copied out a few of my sermons and are passing them around. Perhaps one has fallen into this doctor's hands. What is his name?

J.P. Carl Jung.

BROTHER That is a familiar name. I know a family not far from here by that name. I wonder if. . .

J.P. Excuse me, Brother, but he will live a long time off in the future. There is, however, another idea or suggestion that you and Carl Jung seem to share. Perhaps he also learned it from you. It concerns maturity in one's spiritual life. Jung speaks in a number of instances about the second half of life being almost by necessity the more reflective, introverted, and intuitive; that as one gets older and older, God and religious concerns become more important. Many others during my time speak of a midlife crisis of sorts, a crisis of opportunity that can be a deeply spiritual experience.

BROTHER I believe there are three stages to one's life with God. The first you might call the stage of the spiritual child who is entirely entranced by the wonderful works and revelations of God. This person is overwhelmed by the outpouring of God's goodness into the celestial and terrestrial marvels. The man or woman in this stage feels God flourishing and blossoming. In youthfulness of spirit we are jubilant before so many gifts. The second stage occurs when in many strange ways God seems to withdraw from the soul. Perhaps this is the stage of spiritual poverty. This can be a wild and lonely path. Perhaps this is what you speak of when speaking of midlife. I have often said, even in sermons, that until someone reaches their fortieth year they cannot know real peace, cannot truly know God, no matter how hard they try, and even then it is not until often the fiftieth year that the God-seeing person sinks down, is immersed in, and melted into the simple, pure, divine, and innermost core of their own source. Until the fortieth year people are usually very busy with many things, with the heart being hounded by this impulse or that desire, this humor or that need. When the proper time arrives, however, the maturing spirit begins to ask many upsetting questions, like what direction should my life take, and is there truly a God. This time can be very painful and bitter, but if the person surrenders to the truth that God teaches, he or she will experience the most sublime bliss, where peace is possessed. It is a process of returning to one's source from which all grace flows, of divinizing the soul.

J.P. You shared some beautiful thoughts about the child within each of us in a sermon only last month on the eve of the Epiphany feast. Could you share some of your insights?

BROTHER Oh, yes. I related how the story of the holy family's flight from Bethlehem to Egypt is very much like what happens within each of us as we mature spiritually. You know the story, of course. Joseph is told in a dream by an angel that Herod wished to kill the child Jesus, so Joseph and Mary were to take the child to Egypt where he could grow and mature in wisdom and strength. Is this not what happens in each of us, Father John? Do we not each have a Herod of pride and worldliness within us? Don't we each want to be noticed, held in high regard, perhaps have titles and positions of authority? Don't we each want to impress others by our mere appearance? Of course everyone has different temptations. Some get caught in appearance, others become driven by the gratifications of their senses, while others have a tendency toward this infatuation or that. The Herod of our inner world, whatever form it takes, would very much kill the child within us unless we flee into the ground of our hearts where God dwells. Does not the angel of good conscience and faith warn us when greed is attacking, and will not the Joseph within us, the protector and guardian of faith, safely guide us into the land of growing wisdom and strengthening spirit?

J.P. Jesus, then, is our ideal, our model. That the divine child in us grow in wisdom and strength, bow low before suffering, and submit to God dwelling in us so that we can then end our lives in gracious praise of God rather than in bitterness. Are you saying that what happened to Christ must happen in each of us?

BROTHER Yes, Father John. All we can do ultimately is sit down and say, "God bless you bitterness most bitter. You are full of God's love."

J.P. Brother, you remind me of a story told by a cleric from India who translated an Eastern story. It's a brief story about a man who wished to become a teacher of the truth so he went off to a greater teacher who asked, "Are you prepared to be ignored, ridiculed, and starving until you are 45 years old?" "I am," answered the man, then asked, "What will happen after I am 45?" The teacher answered, "You will grow accustomed to it."

BROTHER That is an appropriate point. I often tell another story of detachment and surrender, which is the one thing necessary to build the inner temple for the Lord to reside. It is a story about an old man who was so profoundly detached from all things and in union with God that he could not remember what things looked like anymore. One day a knock came at the door. The old man answered the door and, of course, the visitor asked for something. The polite old man closed the door, went to get the object asked for but immediately forgot that he had even been asked to get it. The visitor knocked again and the old man answered. Again he made the promise to fetch a certain object from the house but when he closed the door he forgot again. Finally after three attempts the old man said in frustration, "Come into the house and take whatever it is you keep asking for. I can't remember what it looks like anymore as my spirit has become so empty of worldly matters." It seems, Father John, that as we grow older, God helps us become more accustomed to the pains and sufferings of life, growing less concerned with the outer world. By this grace, God helps us become God-seeing. Prayer especially can help build God's temple in the ground of the soul.

J.P. There are just a few other quick questions I wanted to ask before we must conclude this interview.

BROTHER Good, John. I wanted to get into Strasbourg

tonight to see what can be done in complaint to the council. I also wish to visit a friend along the way. His daughter only recently has been inflicted with the plague. Perhaps you would like to go with me to town tonight, Father. Then you can stay overnight here with the Merswins.

J.P. Well, Brother, I have been warned about the city and plague. I would not wish to be infected and to carry it back into my time.

BROTHER Let's not get carried away with this imaginative return into history, Father. Detach from this fantasy for a moment and move on with another question.

J.P. Yes. A question. Something more personal, perhaps.

BROTHER We have only been discussing the most impersonal issue so far, my relationship with God. Is that what you meant to say?

J.P. No, no. Let me ask about your preaching. It has been said that you preach the truth as wholeheartedly as any preacher of your day. I've also heard you called the preacher of preachers. How does such affirmation make you feel?

BROTHER Everyone has their work, and each gift is God-given. Some spin, others make shoes, while others are very good at practical matters. I have often thought that if I were not a priest I would be a shoemaker. I would be happy earning my living with my hands. Regarding the preaching, however. I preach to ordinary, hard-working people. Even when speaking to nuns, I remind them frequently that there are many shoemakers and housewives out in the world who support themselves with very hard work, and pray. That there are poor people who may have to practically break their backs carrying manure to earn enough just to eat. All these people may be a hundred times more successful in their God-seeing spiritual lives than nuns, churchmen, theologians, or myself. We all have our place and gifts. It is, however, the simplicity of one's inner life that determines one's disposition to the ground of the soul where each meets God. God works in diverse and wondrous ways. God is constant, unlike ourselves oftentimes, simple, unlike our tendency to multiply complexity, and divine, for God can work in all and all can be, work, and live in God. There is no task so small that it is not a proof of God's presence. In the final analysis, we are accountable for our work. We must do for our brothers and sisters what they cannot do for themselves. We must each return to our neighbor what we have been graciously given by God. At least, we must try.

J.P. What place does prayer have in this responsibility to let God work through you?

BROTHER Just that. Let God work through you whether you are doing good deeds and exercising care for others, or whether you are ransacking your inner house for the lost coin of union with God. It seems today that everyone wants to be the eye, contemplating all the time, while no one does the work. A person must find the time each day or night to sink into the depths, but each according to his or her choice. If you choose to be an eye of contemplation, fine; if the hand of virtue, also fine. We must above all seek to serve God's will, which will then guide our will. Peace grows out of the inner ground when you submit to God's presence there.

J.P. Would you make suggestions as to how one might pray?

BROTHER No. I am a teacher and preacher with few opinions on how you can sink into the ground of your soul other than to say, leave all but God behind. I am not one of those so-called experts who are pretentious enough after 40 years in religious life to present their theories concerning spiritual exercises and prayer without the slightest notion of what they are talking about. With their judgmental opinions they are much bolder than I. I teach only that when in prayerful devotion, one should always address the Lord. Other than that I will not judge which exercise, which method or technique is best. God's ways are mysterious enough that when those who cling to this or that religious exercise or method die, they will find a very great surprise awaiting them. God will not ask about exercises but will look for the marks of birth in the heart and ground. Therefore, perform only the work and devotions the spirit guides you to do and do all for God. In that is your peace.

J.P. Peace in the kingdom?

BROTHER Yes, peace in the kingdom within. When you

find peace there, sinking into the ground, the innermost depths where the treasures and gifts of God await, then you can turn outward to share this peace with others. God is closer to the soul than the soul is to itself. Look for the kingdom there.

J.P. Before we depart, Brother, I wanted to share one more story with you. We could go further certainly to talk about the philosophical understanding of how God is in, yet beyond the soul, but such a discussion leads to so many varied distinctions. I would like to share, rather, a story which I think captures some images and ideas you present. Stories at times reveal more than philosophy.

BROTHER If it is a good story, perhaps I can borrow it for a future sermon.

J.P. "Once upon a time in a forest, three young trees were growing side by side. As they grew, they shared with one another their dreams of what they would become when they grew up to be big trees. The first tree said, 'My dream is to become part of a luxurious home where many famous people come and go and admire the grain and color of my wood.'

"The second tree said, 'My dream is to become the tall mast of an elegant sailing vessel that journeys to the seven seas.'

"And the third said, 'My dream is to become part of a great tower, so high that it will inspire people who look at it. People will come from all over the world to see it.'

"And so the young trees dreamed. Eventually the trees grew to maturity and were cut down. The first didn't become a part of a luxurious home, as it had dreamed, but instead some of its wood was fashioned into a simple manger, a wooden trough to hold the hay that animals ate. The second tree didn't become the tall mast of an elegant ship, as it had dreamed, but instead it became the sides of an ordinary fishing boat like many others on the Sea of Galilee. The third didn't become part of a tall tower, as it had dreamed, but was fashioned into the beams of a cross and used for crucifixion." [8]

BROTHER Excellent. I will pen a copy in the morning. Only by such emptiness can we become divinized and God-hued so as to birth God, feed our neighbors, and suffer our cross with the hope of Christ. Let us go now, Father. It is getting late. We have work to do.

Johannes Tauler died of the plague on June 16, 1361, the second of four epidemic outbreaks, at the Monastery of St. Nicholas in Undis with his sister, a Dominican nun, by his side. Tauler is highly esteemed for his collection of 84 sermons, which gained great popularity in his lifetime and grew in influence through the centuries. They survive in the form of reports or copied versions, taken by nuns as they listened. It is believed, however, that they represent a high degree of accuracy in comparison to his oral presentations.

Suggested Readings

Johannes Tauler: Sermons, transl. Maria Shrady (The Classics of Western Spirituality). Mahwah, N.J.: Paulist Press, 1985.

An Anthology of Christian Mysticism, ed. with biographical notes by Paul De Jaegher. Springfield, Ill.: Templegate Pub., 1977.

An Introduction to the Medieval Mystics of Europe, ed. Paul E. Szarmach. Albany: State University of N.Y. Press, 1984.

Excerpts from the writings of JOHANNES TAULER

"And for the same reason the human circuit, in its essential meaning, is the noblest and most perfect when it returns again to its source...divine circulation should also be adopted by us if we are to attain spiritual motherhood in our soul. We, too, must completely turn inward in order to go out again."

Sermon 1 Christmas

"What should remain is a pure cleaving to God alone, a making room for Him, Who is the highest and nearest, so that His work can prosper, and His birth can be accomplished without hindrance."

Sermon 1 Christmas

"A proverb says that a child kept too much at home remains uncouth abroad. That holds true of those people who have never left the house of their natural inclinations, who have not gone beyond their nature or beyond all those messages they have received from seeing and hearing, from emotions and excitements....Once their momentary mood and external circumstances change, such people are at their wit's end. They have never overcome their natural selves and so cannot experience this noble birth."

Sermon 1 Christmas

"Herod, who wanted to persecute the Child and kill Him, signifies the world, which would doubtless kill the Child, and we must certainly flee from it if we wish to retain the Child within us. But even when we have fled the world, in an exterior sense, and have retired into our cells and cloisters, there will always be an arch enemy reigning in the soul. A whole world will rise up in us which we will never overcome without constant practice and effort and the help of God. There are strong and fierce foes which will assail us, and to vanquish them is exceedingly hard."

Sermon 2 Epiphany

"The woman then turns her house upside down, searching for the coin. How does this search happen in us? One way is active, in which we are seeking; the other passive, in which we are sought....We seek God exteriorly when we perform pious practices and good works of various kinds as we are admonished or urged by God, and advised by His friends, mostly by exercising virtues such as humility, gentleness, silence, detachment, and all the other virtues which we practice or can practice.

"The other way, however, is more sublime. We must allow ourselves to sink into our ground, into the innermost depth, and seek the Lord there, as He instructed us when he said: 'The Kingdom of God is within you!' Whoever wishes to discover this Kingdom—where God reigns with all His riches in His essence and nature—he must look for it where it is: in the very depth of the soul, where God is infinitely closer to the soul, more inherent, as the soul is to itself."

Sermon 37 Third Sunday after Trinity III

"By this action the soul becomes God-hued, divinized, reformed in the form of God. It possesses everything by grace which God possesses by nature by way of its union with Him and by sinking into Him. Thus the soul soars far above itself, right into the very core of God."

Sermon 37 Third Sunday after Trinity III

Julian of Norwich

(1342 - c. 1417)

It was early April of the year 1400, and I was growing increasingly impatient. There was little fighting going on during what will one day be known as the Hundred Years War, so I was able to visit the great London cathedral of Westminster and spend almost two days at the Old Tithe Barn at Bradford-on-Avon. The more I wandered through the countryside of England, the more I became convinced that I would never get an interview with Lady Julian, the anchoress at the church of Norwich. Despite the efforts of Alice, Lady Julian's serving maid, I was sure the interview would not take place. Anchorites, or hermits as we might call them in our time, were not accustomed to giving out interviews for public consumption. Julian did see selected women or men to give spiritual guidance now and then, especially those recommended by the local bishop under whose support Julian lived the anchorite life in Norwich. The bishop was not on the island during my visit, however. Important matters concerning the continued schism over the papacy had taken him away on church business. Alice was my only hope of getting to talk with Julian. The clergy of the parish of Norwich were very pleased to have Lady Julian's anchorhold rooms attached to the side of the church but they would not interfere when it came to her privacy. Julian had been in the two rooms on the side of the church for over 22 years, having been enclosed there in a ritual ceremony by the bishop, and so the clergy were not going to test Julian's desire for withdrawal by asking her to see an outsider, especially someone who was not from the parish or island, and who spoke such a strange English dialect.

As I entered the parish churchyard of Norwich in East Anglia at the agreed-upon time, I saw Alice come out of a small door far to the right of the church. I wondered as Alice and I greeted one another if that was the door to Julian's anchorhold. Alice was not in the mood for conversation, it seemed, but when she motioned for me to follow, I did without hesitation, ducking through the door from which she had just come. Alice pointed to a chair that stood by a half-opened window in the back wall of what was obviously Alice's kitchen. I opened my note pad to look over some of the quotes I had copied from Lady Julian's book of showings called *Revelations of Divine Love*. There were very few copies available of Julian's writings; in fact, only four or five until almost the twentieth century when translations would abound. As I sat quietly on the kitchen chair, I wondered about this unique woman known as Julian. It was not her real name, it seems, but rather the name of the church to which this kitchen scrub-room was attached. No one knew much about her life previous to her withdrawal here. No one knew her name, whether or not she had ever been married, had children, or if she had been a nun in some other convent. I wanted to ask

Alice if she knew much about Julian's life, especially during the time of her transforming vision after a terrible illness in May 1373, some 27 years ago, but Alice was busy at work preparing a meal. Just as I thought of my own hunger with lunchtime drawing near and having had no breakfast, I heard the dust of a voice rise from behind the wooden-covered window just next to my chair. The shutter was open a few inches but not enough for me to see anything clearly. From the sound of the voice it seemed that Lady Julian, if that is who it was, was sitting exactly as I was, sideways to the wall, yet on the other side. I would not be able to see her unless I not only opened the door window but also poked my head through.

J.P. Is it Lady Julian who addresses me?

JULIAN Yes, it is. It may take me a few moments to understand your odd English speech but I shall try. I am unlettered and somewhat ignorant and have not heard your dialect before. Alice tells me you are a priest from a country that speaks my language. It sounds rather harsh indeed. Say something else, priest.

J.P. Having seen some of your writings, I wonder about your claim to be uneducated. I can't imagine how you could write one of the most beautiful books in the English language, as you have, without having a full background of studies. Your book of revelations stands out in the history of literature as a masterpiece of English development and usage.

JULIAN I said I was ignorant of letters, not of study and reflection. Since the Lord first pleased to show me the oneness of himself and his marvelous love for me in my early seeings of God, I have tried to come to understand these showings in a fuller way. In fact, I only recently completed the longer version of my writings. I pray my continued studies and thought have helped me prepare a writing that will truly show forth the Lord's love for all creatures and that will be an aid for all women and men of my time who desire to be lovers of Christ. God longs to teach us how to know and love him. He longs to bring us to bliss. Whatever I have written, may it bring me more fully to the God who loved me and you before time began.

J.P. I certainly want, Julian, to pick up on the themes you have already mentioned; God's love and oneing of us and creation, for example, but first I wanted to ask about your background. All we know from your writings is that you had a vision when coming out of a life-threatening illness when only 30 years old, that you had prayed as a child for three gifts from God, and that you seem to have loved your own mother deeply. I gather your mother was by your side as God showed you himself in these visions or showings as you call them. Could you tell us a bit more of your background?

JULIAN Before I came to this church, I had another name. Now I am only a weak and frail woman who has withdrawn to be one with God in prayer and love.

J.P. You may be weak and frail physically, my Lady, but you have more strength than I or many men would ever have. To live the life you do in this hermitage and to write with confidence what you have seen of God while living in a society that does not place a high regard on much other than ritual religion, would demand great strength of substance.

JULIAN It is God who strengthens my body and soul, oneing me with healing salve, but I would rather not talk about who I was but who I am in God.

J.P. And who are you in God, Lady Julian?

JULIAN Our Lord God has shown me many secrets, some great, some small, but secrets still, not because God made them so but because in our blindness and ignorance they remain hidden. God has great tenderness and wants us to understand him. He reveals all of himself out of love. First, God wants us to understand that the most noble thing he has ever made is humankind. There is no creature made by God that can fully know how much, how tenderly, and how sweetly

God, our creator Lord, loves us. God is absolutely everything that is good, and the very goodness that everything possesses is God.

J.P. When I spoke recently to one Meister Eckhart, he spoke of God as an "Is-ness." You speak of God as Goodness.

JULIAN Correct. When I saw God in my showings, I saw God in a single point. This means to me that God is in all things. God also showed himself to me as though he were a pilgrim here on earth leading us back to his heavenly bliss. God showed himself to me as one reigning in goodness and nature in our souls, his resting place, his holy city from which he can never be removed. Our soul is made by God to be his dwelling place and the dwelling place for our soul is God who, of course, is un-made. God is truly, young priest, the ground, the teaching, the substance, the purpose, the ultimate reward for which all our souls seek. Shall I share more of what God has shown of who he is, or is that too much for your understanding?

J.P. No. Please go on. I can hear in what you are saying the themes of other mystics whom I have recently interviewed and who also have a very profound sense that God is present in creation and humanity in a way that is both complete in its sense of unity, yet somehow differentiating as well. I know this is a delicate problem because you cannot say that creation is God because that would be pantheism, nor do you want to dualistically cut God off from creation so you have a problem in how to capture this sense of being one, yet two.

JULIAN God showed me that we are all of God, to speak right to the heart of your concern. That is what we are. No matter how we might feel, whether happy or sad, God wants us to understand and to know by faith that we are in a sense more truly in heaven than we are on earth. Let me put it another way. In God's showings I saw no difference between God and our substance. It seemed to be all of God. What this means to me is that our substance is in God. God is God, and our substance a creature in God.

Both our substance and sensuality, together and "oned,"

may correctly be called our soul. Our sensuality is the beautiful city in which Jesus rests enclosed, while our substance is the same nature as Jesus and is enclosed in him as he sits in the Godhead.

J.P. Out of your experience of God you came to understand that God is Goodness itself, creates all out of good and puts goodness into all, that God is the one point, and the "oneing" of our body and soul into a glorious union.

JULIAN So far you are correct. The God of my showings is the love that gives and binds me and you and all men and women and all creation together, for we are one in each other.

J.P. When I first read parts of your manuscript of revelations, I was struck by the sense of a creative community. That God is in trinity, overflowing into creation and each of us. Your sense of the kinship of all reality gives me an image of God and all the universe as family, oned by blood but with differences.

JULIAN We were all created at the same time, so your image that we are kin is very appropriate. I like to say that we were all knit and oned with God. Perhaps the body would be a good image to use here. As we cover our bodies with clothing and as the muscles are covered with skin, and the bones then with muscles, and then even the heart with the chest, so are we, soul and body, covered and clothed with the goodness of God.

J.P. One of your most popular little stories, Lady Julian, at least one of the most referred to in my time, is the one about a hazel nut.

JULIAN Oh, yes. This little showing tells us of what you call kinship, Reverend, and what I call the oneing of God's love for all. In this showing, God somehow placed in the palm of my hand a hazelnut, the size of a little round ball. I looked at the odd little nut with my inner eye of invitation and said, "What is it?" God quickly answered saying, "It is everything that is created." Looking at the small nut in my hand, I wondered how it could possibly survive without crumbling into dust. That answer also came from the God who said, "It lives now and will live because I love it." You see, Father John, everything has and continues in being because God loves it.

J.P. Maybe at this point I can bring up one of your showings that many people of my time find disagreeable to talk about. Now I have traveled a bit and seen rather different attitudes toward the biological necessity of cleansing the body of human waste, but you bring even this into God's realm.

JULIAN Absolutely. I don't know about your culture. Perhaps you have an unusual embarrassment about the body and its functions, but I believe that God permeates us even into our lowest or humblest need. God never disdains creation nor would God refuse to serve us in the simplest function of our bodies in nature.

J.P. I wanted to give you a chance to make that point, Lady Julian, even if it surprises some people.

JULIAN Does God not take delight in the image he created, in all its function and beauty?

J.P. Oh yes. I am not taking exception at all to God's delight or even sense of humor. I would, however, like to ask another question. It refers to a point I made earlier when I said that when I read your revelations, I got a clear image of God as family or community. This is because you speak of God with so many images and metaphors.

JULIAN God is one and "oneing," as I said earlier. God is trinity and can I say "trinitying"?

J.P. It's your language, Lady Julian. I don't know if the word will stick, but how do you use it?

JULIAN I mean that in God there are the three properties of life, love, and light. Is God not always creating these in ever-newness? That is what I mean.

J.P. I understand. Who else is this God I referred to as a family?

JULIAN I will tell you what God said in a showing to me. God said, "I am this—the goodness of the father, I am the wisdom of the mother, the light and grace, the trinity, the unity. I am the royal goodness of all things. I am what makes you love, long, and desire, and I am the fulfillment of all you desire." In other showings God reveals himself as teacher, womb, nurse, pilgrim, nurturer, comforter, brother, sister, and savior. As the oldest testament tells us, God is wisdom, "the mother of all good things," (Wisdom 7:11-12). In the New Testament, Jesus is the "spiritual food" and "drink" (1 Corinthians 10:3-4), for we are "as eager for milk as newborn babies. . . pure milk of the spirit to make you grow into salvation, now that you have tasted that the Lord is good" (1 Peter 2:2-3). Would you like me to continue, Father John?

J.P. With these few biblical references, would you tell us what might be one of your most favorite references to God? I presume it is the image of God as mother?

JULIAN I speak often of God in my writings as the mother who nurtures and feeds. I do not make mention in my showings but Alice, my serving assistant, likes very much the sentence from St. Anselm's *Prayers and Meditations.* Let me quote what this great mystic of the church prays when addressing Christ. "Do, mother of my soul... what the mother of my flesh would do." [9] Isn't that beautiful, Father John?

J.P. It is, Lady. Perhaps one of the primary reasons your profound revelations are so much more popular in my day than even in your own is because of your imagery of God as mother.

JULIAN I find that God becomes real to me as mother. God is showing us even now that in God's womb we are enclosed and grow, that it is God who gives birth to us, feeding us from the side of Jesus, teaching us, caring for us as we grow, washing, forgiving, healing us with a constant tender touch even unto our death when we will be reborn into the womb of God. From source to source is the mother's love. No one person has the ability or could ever know how to do all this except God alone.

J.P. When you speak of God as mother, are you referring to Jesus?

JULIAN All mothers bear us to pain, but who only to the full? Our mother Jesus. Only Jesus bears us to everlasting joy in the kingdom.

J.P. Lady Julian, you are not the first I have interviewed who has said that Jesus is mother, birthing yet, even, it seems, through the cross. Perhaps we can return to the image of the cross a bit later because it is primary to your showing, but I wanted to ask you further about this mother image of Jesus. I know that there is Scripture foundation, a few you've given already, as well as a long tradition through St. Clement, St. John Chrysostom, St. Ambrose, St. Anselm, even St. Augustine, and others who have used the image of God the mother or mother hen, but you weave it through your revelations in a way no one else has or will, as far as I can see. My question concerns a complaint by some in my time who feel you may be feminizing God or Jesus too much and perhaps thereby sentimentalizing Jesus. There is even a play being staged in my time taking your words and acting them out, which a critic has said makes Christ rather effeminate.

JULIAN Feminizing God, you say. Making Christ effeminate, you say. Sentimentalizing Jesus, you say. My young friend, I do not make God, God makes me. I do not feminize or masculinize God. God does such to me and you. Christ is not like my mother; no, my mother is like Christ. Christ does not imitate me or you, we imitate Christ. Whatever goodness there is in nature is first because God is. God is the true father and mother of nature from which all that is made flows. Now I understand three ways of seeing motherhood in God. The first is grounded in the making of our natures, for God has certainly created each of us, man and woman. Second I see God's motherhood in God's choosing to take on our nature, which was before the beginning, in a motherhood of grace. And thirdly, the motherhood of God is working. I am sorry if those who criticize believe I overemphasize, but as I said I am unlettered and if these people are closer to God, surer and steadier in their understanding of God's love for them, then I would like to hear them teach me of God's great love. Perhaps the Lord has shown them an understanding I have not seen. I would be delighted to learn. In the showings God has given me, I see God as maternal goodness and Jesus as that healing, touching, and embracing God. I do not believe I am wrong in seeing Jesus as mother.

J.P. No, Lady Julian, I believe it is the criticism of your feminine language for God that is exaggerated. Such criticism indicates a continued inability to see God as anything more than a projection of self. You do not have to defend the one point of God or your experience that God is mother. There will be many in my time who will thank you for expanding their understanding of God. You've just reminded me, Lady Julian, of something. Let's see if I can remember if it was Mechtild or Hildegard of Bingen who said something like this: "Without woman, man could not be called man; without man, woman could not be named woman...neither could ever live without the other."

JULIAN I believe it was Hildegard who said that.

J.P. In the light of some of the criticism about your God language, I wanted also to share with you something said about you by perhaps the greatest mystic of my time, noted for his authorship and publications. His name is Brother Thomas Merton and he writes in his book, *Seeds of Destruction*:

> Julian is without doubt one of the most wonderful of all Christian voices. She gets greater and greater in my eyes as I grow older, and whereas in the old days I used to be crazy for St. John of the Cross, I would not exchange him now for Julian if you gave me the world and the Indies and all the Spanish mystics rolled up in one bundle. I think that Julian of Norwich is with Newman, the greatest English theologian. She is really that. For she reasons from her experience of the substantial center of the great Christian mystery of redemption. She gives her experience and her deductions, clearly, separating the two. And the experience is of course nothing merely subjective. It is the objective mystery of Christ as apprehended by her, with the mind and formation of a fourteenth-century English woman. And that four-

teenth-century England is to me and always has been a world of light.[10]

JULIAN I am deeply honored by Brother Merton's compliments. I do not know this St. John of the Cross but I would very much like to. Could you perhaps seek out some of his writings for me?

J.P. I would very much like to, but he has not yet been born.

JULIAN Oh yes, God has not yet given him birth.

J.P. I will be speaking shortly with Teresa of Avila, a spiritual companion of St. John's. I will make known your interest.

JULIAN Thank you.

J.P. Perhaps we could go on, Lady Julian, into an area that has caused you some difficulties. Thus far your showings have been filled with a deep sense of awe at the wonders of God's love for all creation. You do, however, eventually in your writings deal with sin. In fact, I believe this subject has taken a larger part in the second and longer version of your showings.

JULIAN You are correct. When I first experienced God, even when I saw Jesus on the Cross, I could see nothing but love for me and humanity. I could not see sin. In fact, for some time I thought of sin as a nothing. It could not have existence in this goodness we call creation, for all but sin is created in God.

J.P. How did you reconcile the fact that it does exist, that there are great acts of separation, division, blindness, breaking apart, "un-oneing" from God? How did you deal over these past 20 years with the reality that at times, and far more often than we would like, a part of ourselves—our needs, angers, jealousy, thoughts, desires, imaginings, bodies—attempts to take over the whole of ourselves, dividing us from kinship with God and creation?

JULIAN Stories are best in situations when paradox abounds. I tell the story of a servant who is one day sent out by the Master, meaning of course the love of God, and who runs immediately to do the Master's will. Without warning, however, he falls headlong into a ravine. It was an accident, yet the servant whom the Master wanted to help was so confused and hurt from the fall that he became blind to the loving Lord who stooped over to lift him gently. Let me tell you, Father John, that if I were to do nothing but sin, rejecting God at every turn, my sin would still not stop God from bending down to lift me with his goodness. This does not mean that we are free to go about sinning — our task is to cleave to God's goodness. If we fall, however, the Lord is present there to work through even that suffering.

J.P. You remind me of another story, Lady Julian, about the Christian's journey. A child once asked a wise abbess what happened on the journey to God. The abbess looked at the child and said, "Well, on the road to God you fall down and get up, fall down and get up, fall down and get up again." "Well," said the child, "what happens if you fall down on the road and cannot get up again?" The abbess responded, "We call that Hell." And with eyes wide open the child asks, "What if you never trip and fall on this road?" "Well, my child," said the abbess, "we call that heaven."

JULIAN Your story shows me God's love again. God is only forgiveness. God wants us, however, to forgive our own sins rather than remaining bent low, to stand up to look into the glory of Christ's face without accusing ourselves too much. It seems life is all about seeing God and then not, seeing God and failing to again, but God says, "I love you and you love me and our love can never divide us." God allows sin to cause our fall against our will and love, but God promises to take care and to lead us to the fullness of our home, where we can share again the joy we were once given and can experience again. I understand that in this life we hang on a cross dying with Jesus in pain and passion but Jesus shall call us home to the kingdom, the beautiful city and dwelling place of our souls where he rests with joy. God never said that we won't be tempted or have to work hard to keep on our feet, to continue your story, nor did God say we would not be terribly troubled at times. God does say, however, that even in all this we will not be overcome.

J.P. Your message is so remarkably hopeful. It is almost too much hope to bear.

JULIAN Ah, yes, we can understand a God of power, or a God who is wisdom and sees our every action, but a God who is all love and is willing to suffer on the cross or even further, if necessary, is too much for us, it seems. It is God's wish and will that you accept the joy and bliss he gives you, the home that has always been yours. If you realize now that it is you who are the home and kingdom of our Lord, then you shall be made like him and forever "oned" to him in peace and rest. This is what God wants for each of us and all creation. Is that not enough and too much?

J.P. May I conclude this discussion, Lady, by repeating what has become your most often quoted sentence?

JULIAN Surely. I would be happy to know what your time needs so much to hear that you would say it is quoted.

J.P. "All will be well, and every manner of thing will be well."

JULIAN Thank you, Father. We need to hear such hopeful words often. Please, Alice, would you give Father something to eat before his journey.

ALICE Yes, Lady Julian. Do you continue your fast?

JULIAN Yes, thank you, Alice. Goodbye, Father John.

J.P. Yes, thank you again. Lady Julian, can I ask one more brief question?

JULIAN Certainly.

J.P. Why do you fast from food?

JULIAN That all may be well.

Lady Julian of Norwich remained in her anchorhold until her death, estimated to have occurred between 1420 and 1429 when it is believed a male anchorite moved into the anchor rooms attached to the Norwich church. Julian was the first woman to write a book in the English language, of which there are two versions, the short and long text of *The Revelations of Divine Love.*

Suggested Readings

Julian: Woman of Our Day, ed. Robert Llewelyn. Mystic, Conn.: Twenty-Third Publications, 1987.

The Divine Revelations of Divine Love of Julian of Norwich, transl. James Walsh, S.J. New York: Harper & Brothers, Inc., 1961.

Julian of Norwich: Showings, ed. and transl. Edmund Colledge, O.S.A. and James Walsh, S.J. (Classics of Western Spirituality Series). Mahwah, N.J.: Paulist Press, 1978.

"God Is Our Mother": Julian of Norwich and the Medieval Image of Christian Feminine Divinty, by Jennifer P. Heinnel (Elizabethan & Renaissance Studies, ed. Dr. James Hogg, 92:5). Institut für Anglistik und Amerikanistik, Universitat Salzburg, Austria.

Meditations with Julian of Norwich, introd. and versions by Brendan Doyle. Santa Fe, N.M.: Bear & Co., 1983.

Who Was Julian? A Beginners Guide, Michael McLean. Julian Shrine, All Hallows, Roven Road, Norwich, England.

"A Lesson of Love": The Revelations of Julian of Norwich, ed. and transl. for devotional use by Father John-Julian, O.J.N. New York: Walker and Company, 1988.

"Julian of Norwich:" Reflections on Selected Texts, by Austin Cooper, O.M.I. Mystic, Conn.: Twenty-Third Publications, 1988.

Excerpts
from the writings of
JULIAN OF NORWICH

"For the Trinity is God, God is the Trinity; the Trinity is our Maker, the Trinity is our Keeper, the Trinity is our everlasting Lover, the Trinity is our endless Joy and Bliss, by our Lord Jesus Christ."

A Lesson of Love: The Revelations of Julian of Norwich
Revelation 4

"Also in this revelation He showed me a little thing, the size of a hazel nut in the palm of my hand, and it was as round as a ball. I looked at it with the eye of my understanding and thought: 'What can this be?' And it was generally answered thus: 'It is all that is made'.... In this little thing I saw three characteristics: the first is that God made it, the second is that God loves it, the third that God keeps it. But what did I observe in that? Truly the Maker, the Lover, and the Keeper for, until I am in essence united to Him, I can never have full rest nor true joy...."

A Lesson of Love: The Revelations of Julian of Norwich
Revelation 5

"For as the body is clad in the clothes, and the flesh in the skin, and the bones in the flesh, and the heart in the breast, so are we, soul and body, clad in the goodness of God and enclosed—yea, and even more intimately, because all these others may waste and wear away, but the goodness of God is ever whole, and nearer to us without any comparison."

A Lesson of Love: The Revelations of Julian of Norwich
Revelation 6

"But Jesus (who in this vision told me of all that I needed) answered by this word and said: 'Sin is inevitable, but all shall be well, and all shall be well, and all manner of thing shall be well."

A Lesson of Love; The Revelations of Julian of Norwich
Revelation 27

"Thus in our creation, God All Power is our natural Father, and God All Wisdom is our natural Mother, with the Love and the Goodness of the Holy Spirit—who is all one God, one Lord. And in the knitting and in the oneing, He is our most true Spouse, and we are His beloved Wife and His fair Maiden. With this Wife He is never displeased, for he says: 'I love thee and thou lovest me, and our love shall never be separated in two.'"

A Lesson of Love: The Revelations of Julian of Norwich
Revelation 58

"Thus in our true Mother, Jesus, our life is grounded, in His own for seeing Wisdom from without beginning, with the high power of the Father and the high supreme Goodness of the Holy Spirit."

A Lesson of Love; The Revelations of Julian of Norwich
Revelation 63

"He said not 'Thou shalt not be tempted; thou shalt not be troubled; thou shalt not be distressed' but He said, 'Thou shalt not be overcome.'"

A Lesson of Love: The Revelations of Julian of Norwich
Revelation 68

"And all this was shown in spiritual understanding, He saying these words: 'I keep thee full safely.' ...But this was shown: that whether in falling or rising we are ever preciously protected in one love. In the sight of God we do not fall; in the sight of self we do not stand—and both of these are true as I see it, but the way our Lord God sees it is the highest truth.

A Lesson of Love: The Revelations of Julian of Norwich
Revelation 82

Teresa of Avila

(Teresa of Jesus)

(1515 - 1582)

My letter of introduction to Mother Teresa arrived in Madrid from Father Jerome Gracian, her confessor, spirited supporter, and Carmelite visitor, a few days after Christmas, 1577, just in time for me to travel quickly northwest to the town of Avilia in the Castile district of central Spain. It was there that Teresa had been born on March 28, 1515, where she was educated, and where she had founded her first community of Discalced (unshod) reformed Carmelites in 1562, now known as St. Joseph's convent.

Teresa had joined the Carmelite religious community in Avila when she was only 20 years old and had suffered a life-threatening illness a few years later. She was overwhelmed by struggles regarding her life of easy prayer and comfortable Carmelite religious living until she was 39, when she chose to begin a new life of dedication to God by living a more primitive rule of Carmel. It was through her struggles that she was called to be a reformer, establishing eleven new convents of Barefoot Carmelites by 1577, and an author, writing *The Book of Her Life* in 1562, held now by inquisitioners who thought it possibly heretical, *The Way of Perfection* in 1565, and the book just completed only weeks before my visit to Avila on January 5, 1578, *The Dwelling Places*, or Interior Castle as we will call it in the future.

From Fr. Gracian's cover letter, I knew Mother Teresa was in some turmoil as I traveled to Avila for my visit. The reform movement among the Carmelites was not going as smoothly as Teresa had prayed for. In fact it was only a month before my visit that two of her reforming priests, her close soul-companion, Fray Juan de la Cruz (John of the Cross) and Father German had been forcibly kidnapped by Calced Friars in Toledo. The political situation between feuding Carmelite communities not only involved King Philip II, numerous papal nuncios, general visitators, and inquisitioners, but had broken into violence at the kidnapping of these faithful followers of Carmel.

Now in self-imposed seclusion at St. Joseph convent in Avila, Teresa waited anxiously for word concerning the health and whereabouts of her brothers. Father Gracian also mentioned in his letter that Teresa had been vigorously working on a manuscript late in the evenings only five months before while staying in Toledo, so he assumed since she was an aggressive woman with a pen, even at age 62, she would have completed this work by now, no matter how much other correspondence she was obligated to continue with her various convents. Father Gracian suggested I ask Mother about her new book.

As I sat in the visitor's parlor of the Avila Carmel, with letter in hand, I wondered how Teresa could continue the battle within her own community and church without allowing hostility or skepticism to overwhelm her. Certainly she must feel deeply wounded by the disappearance of Fray John, wondering if he were alive or dead or if the rumors were true that he had been beaten and imprisoned by other Carmelite friars.

With a flurry of activity, I was awakened out of my musings to see two nuns enter the parlor, wearing long white cloaks with black veils pulled over their faces. I could barely make out their size or appearance because they remained securely behind a tightly meshed grillwork that divided the room in half. The grillwork was so tightly woven that even without the veils I would have had trouble discerning any special facial features of those masked nuns behind the grille.

It was then that one of the nuns spoke with a warm and lighthearted tone, welcoming me to this community of Carmel. I was delighted to hear Mother Teresa's peaceful voice, knowing then that I was not burdening her further with my visit.

MOTHER I am pleased you were able to join us today, Father John. Father Gracian has informed me that you come from the New World and the future. I am quite pleased to meet you. I have asked Sister Maria to join us for our visit, to take notes if that is all right with you. I broke my arm Christmas night and am unable to do some things for myself these days. Maria will make a copy of these notes for you if you like and can remain in Avila a few days.

J.P. Thank you, Mother. That would be helpful. I'm sorry about the arm and about your companion, John of the Cross.

MOTHER Oh, the arm will heal. It is unimportant. It is sad, however, what the Carmelites have done to John in Toledo. If only I had stayed in that city months back. Perhaps I could have done something. I will not forget the day when we heard he had been kidnapped. I was about to guide some of our younger sisters on a brief pilgrimage to see the work of an artist at work in a church not far from the convent. I believe the people called him El Greco. Well, we never took the trip, for as soon as word came about Fray John, we went to the chapel to pray. Then I set about writing fierce letters to denounce such terrible behavior. I pray that this fracture in our Carmelite community will also heal and that John and German will be returned to us. But, Father, you have not come to speak of those things. Tell me of your new world. I am curious to know where you come from. There has been recent news among some Jesuit brothers that a few of their missionaries to the land called Florida were martyred just a few years ago. We pray often that the new settlement of La Navidad on the island [Haiti] off Florida will grow strong. Master Columbus prays that the Christian community will grow healthy there in time. Do you come from this Florida country?

J.P. Not exactly, Mother. I come from an area called New England. It is considerably north of Florida.

MOTHER Interesting. Why would you call your land New England? Was it not discovered and claimed by Spain and therefore properly called New Spain?

J.P. No, Mother, my land was not founded by Spain. The history gets somewhat complicated. I mean the future gets complex. Can we change the subject, Mother?

MOTHER It is good to learn that others are setting sail, as Master Columbus, to bring the message of Christ to new lands. Now tell me how life is in your future of over 400 years hence. Is there great love for God and church? Do many make the journey to meet the king?

J.P. Well, Mother, much has changed in these years. The church, for example, is not so directly involved in the political desire to capture lands or burn heretics, at least not in the physical sense. The church has spread throughout the world, but it no longer rules kings, presidents, or dictators, as it once did. There has been a negotiated separation in most countries between church and state, although recently in the Moslem countries there has been a return to religious rule of the state. There have been many periods of reform over the years. In fact, only 20 some years ago, in my history, there was a great reform through what we call the Second Vatican Council. It has similarities with your recent Council of Trent.

MOTHER Ah, yes. We are especially having trouble with the Lutheran teachings out of the German lands. How has Luther's heresy fared?

J.P. Well, Mother, new and more open dialogues continue with the Lutheran communities. The Roman church has known its share of schism these last 400 years. In fact, we have just recently had a schism in France.

MOTHER Such occurrences are sad.

J.P. Yes, Mother. We humans are a tenacious lot, always trying to prove that it is our time that will not repeat history. God, however, continues to rain on the just and unjust, although our rain may be a bit more contaminated by acid.

MOTHER God is contaminated by acid?

J.P. No, Mother. Not God, the rain.

MOTHER I do not find any image more appropriate to explain the experience of God than through the downpouring of rain. I often speak of God as our Father, Master, the pattern of our lives, and Christ as the Divine Guest, Companion, Friend, Spouse, and Teacher of our souls, but I am especially fond of this element water when speaking of God's ways. I have spent much time observing it, for it reveals some of the secrets of God. We can see in the life of prayer two founts of water with two troughs. The two troughs of living water are filled, however, in two different ways. The first is filled when we work to know God by building canals of recollection and aqueducts of prayer, and the second is filled with water directly from the spring of God's love and needs no work on our part. In the first trough the water of prayer flows from us and ends with God; while in the second the water flows from the source of God and ends in us. The rain of God forever falls and flows into streams and springs, eventually to form waves that can lift the little boat of our soul, pushing it out further into the ocean of God's love. The secret of how God controls the flow of the waters of peace so that it will not go out of its boundaries but will quench and move in God's purpose causes me to marvel.

I often tell people when they complain that the tension of their lives is too great to go somewhere where they can see the sky and walk a bit.

J.P. Mother, while looking over some material in preparation for our visit today, I stayed in a Benedictine abbey in a state called New Hampshire. During my stay there we had a good deal of rain. There was one storm, however, that soaked and stained all the benches on one side of the church choir. That driving rain moved me to reach for a quote from a great mystic of my 1960s and 1970s history. This Brother Thomas Merton was lettered in theology and philosophy, yet was simple enough to tell the following story about the rain in his book, *Raids on the Unspeakable*:

> I came up here from the monastery last night, sloshing through the cornfield, said vespers, and put some oatmeal on the Coleman stove for supper. It boiled over while I was listening to the rain and toasting a piece of bread at the log fire. The night became very dark. The rain surrounded the whole cabin with its enormous virginal myth, a whole world of meaning, of secrecy, of silence, of rumor. Think of it: all that speech pouring down, selling nothing, judging nobody, drenching the thick mulch of dead leaves, soaking the trees, filling the gullies and crannies of the wood with water, washing out the places where men have stripped the hillside! What a thing it is to sit absolutely alone in the forest at night cherished by this wonderful, unintelligible, perfectly innocent speech, the most comforting speech in the world, the talk that rain makes by itself all over the ridges, and the talk of the water courses everywhere in the hollows.
>
> Nobody started it, nobody is going to stop it. It will talk as long as it wants, this rain. As long as it talks I am going to listen.[11]

MOTHER I do not understand the rain, but I know it speaks of God, as your Merton knows. Every created thing tells us something of God, even an ant. I may not understand some things with intellect, but I know that if we love much, God will rain to overflowing, filling our human natures with delights and peace beyond compare. It is not so important that we think a great deal about God but that we come to love the springs of God's flowing love. It is God who continually sends the waters of peace and quiet in the very interior parts of ourselves. Your Merton knew this, for that is where he listened for God, in himself. Your Merton friend was very much at ease in his little cabin, his house, his castle, enough at ease to listen to his soul as it beat with the rain of God. Could there be anything sadder than to be uncomfortable in your own house, especially when it rains from the source? We are indeed foolish people when we do not listen to the king within the castle of our soul. Do you know of this ignorance in your time, Father John?

J.P. Only from personal experience.

MOTHER What real hope do we have, Father, of finding rest outside of ourselves if we cannot find it first within? Peace and rest flow from within outward, not outward in. We must come to understand what the soul truly wants, to be with God. We stupidly strive to know ourselves while at the same time limiting who we are to these rough bodies of ours. We have heard perhaps that we have souls but seldom do we consider who dwells in the soul. All our attention is taken up with appearances, with the outer walls of the castle, with the dullness of the diamond's setting, with these bodies of ours. It is self-reliance that destroys us. It has almost destroyed me. If we don't want to be slaves to appearance, vanity, self-importance, we must flee from all for the love of All.

J.P. What is the purpose of this self-knowledge?

MOTHER To be united with God, of course. That is the purpose of life itself. To live with him always present and living. How few there are who reach this union, even among those who are careful not to offend God and who have prayed a bit. There are those who think that is enough. The worms of self-love, self-esteem, and judging one's neighbors harshly, crawl into the plant to eat away at the roots. Our goal and treasure is to seek God in the center of the soul. Many books on prayer tell us where we are to find God, within ourselves. Clearly that is the best place to look. It is sad to see the many who remain at the bottom of the mountain, refusing to seek God within, to pray in earnest, and to love with courage.

It also disturbs me that there are some who are so spiritual that, no matter what, they want perfect contemplation in prayer. I say, pray now, however you might. Use books and devotions if you must but pray, pray so you can serve. Do not wait for perfection in prayer. Leave such to God.

J.P. I cannot help but think of the many in my time who would resonate to some of what you are saying about human identity being found not in the transitory but in the enduring mystery of aliveness that lives within. I find, though, that there are many who also misunderstand this self-knowledge, or at least do not go far enough. They may seek to know how they feel, but then they merely follow their feelings. Getting in touch with yourself is big business in my day.

MOTHER It is not a business at all, and I do not speak of merely getting in touch with yourself. I speak of the soul that is touched by God's love to the point where the love of all else falls away without suffering. I speak of union with God who lives within the higher soul, the dwelling and resting place of God. It is a terrible pity how little we know or understand about our deepest and highest souls, the who of who we are.

J.P. You are saying, Mother, that soul or spirit is who we are, not merely body or personality, although these are good in God's eyes. We are then the essence or essential aspect, the ground or spark, the child at home.

MOTHER Yes. The highest value of soul and God are inseparable; the image of God created by God—that is who we are.

J.P. Could you say that soul or spirit is who we are, and body and personality is how and what we are?

MOTHER Yes, I think so. We have probably both experienced great trials in prayer at one time or another, Father, for our spirits may be enslaved prisoners, chained to a thousand vanities. It is the soul that knows that everything other than loving and pleasing God is nothing at all in comparison. It is the soul that knows that real self-knowledge and identity come through knowing God.

J.P. The purpose of self-knowledge for you is quite clear then. Self-knowing is for God-knowing and self-transcendence. This point has been made quite forcibly for me by Maggie Ross, an exceptional spiritual author, in her book *The Fire and the Furnance.* Let me share a quote with you, Mother, about the purpose of self-knowledge.

> We need to read the ancients again and again. We need the light they left behind as we follow them in this divine spelunking [cave searching]. But we need most of all to recover what they most wanted to teach: that the whole point of the journey in the fiery love of God is self-forgetfulness, a self-forgetfulness evolving from a self-awareness that gradually drops away as we become ever-more found in the adoration of God in whom we find our true selves. This movement toward completion no longer needs self-reflection, but needs to be aware only of God. This is true joy: not the emotions, feelings and "experiences" we usually call by those names and contrive, connive, and compete impotently to achieve. We cannot achieve joy. It, too, is a gift—a gift that comes with our evolution toward simplicity in our diversity.[12]

MOTHER Well, having quoted such cleverly written words, our visit is ended. Of course, you did not mean to refer to me as one of the ancients, did you? I have much work to do before I can be called an ancient, even if it is a compliment.

J.P. I'm sorry, Mother, I didn't mean to....

MOTHER Hush, I'm only joking. This Maggie Ross

speaks so beautifully of the delicious fruit of forgetfulness of self and of all things. God never tires of giving us joy, rest, and union. We must not grow tired of receiving these gifts. God and his love is always stirring, for it is unable to contain itself, loving us to himself. It is our task to pray and take up the journey that will lead us to the king who dwells in the center of our castle.

J.P. You have mentioned again what is, I gather, the primary image for the spiritual journey in the book you have been writing recently under Father Gracian's direction.

MOTHER Ah, Father Gracian has told you of my little book. I have just finished it. I do not understand why Father Gracian wanted me to write on such spiritual matters. I told him that I was not as learned as many others and that there already seem to be enough books on prayer. I do not have the intellect that understands such things, if it understands at all. It seems to me that if the intellect does understand it doesn't understand how it understands, at least I don't think it can fully comprehend anything of what it understands. Do you understand?

J.P. Well, I...

MOTHER Please, Father, I am just trying to say that I am not meant for writing. I have neither the health nor the wits for it.

J.P. Now I understand. When I write, Mother, and certainly I do not compare our works, I try to hold onto the thought that my writing does not express so much what I know but rather what I am becoming. Or better yet, Mother, when I feel writing has become a terminal illness, that at any moment will take my life, I hunt for a prayer by a man named Barry Longyear. It goes like this:

> God, grant me inspiration, relieve me of expectation, quiet that voice in me for which nothing is good enough. When I do research, lead me to the answers. When I plan, show me the path. When I write, allow me to enter in and live my story. And when the sto-

ry is done, clear it and its future from my mind. If material success should come my way, remind me to thank you. However, if the only reward I obtain for my writing is the writing itself, let it be sufficient. [13]

MOTHER Actually, Father John, my complaints to Father Gracian were said with some sarcasm for when I actually begin to write, even with headaches and heavy burdens, I do not have enough hands to write fast enough. I lose many thoughts that way. I do, however, feel at times inadequate for the task. I don't know Latin or many technical spiritual terms, and at times I actually get lost in what I am saying. With courageous thoughts, however, the end produces courageous deeds. I wrote this humble book for my sisters in community. They will understand what I have written if they have taken their task of prayer to heart. When I pray, I speak, for God is always close enough to hear. I do not need wings to find God, for all I need do is go into solitude and look at him within myself. When we give ourselves completely to him, so he gives himself completely saying, "Seek me in thee." When I write, I also pray. When I began *The Dwelling Places* last June on the eve of the Feast of the Holy Trinity, I prayed that God would continue to be merciful, for he had helped me do even more difficult things than write a book, and I knew he would do this work for me. I must admit the book brings me happiness. The work and difficulties were worth it.

J.P. Can you describe the labyrinth journey into the castle? It is an imaginative story that articulates the inner journey to health and holiness for many of my time.

MOTHER The journey of prayer is not an easy one, Father. There have been days that I felt like running away from the church when on my way to prayer. However, for those who have not begun, let them enter within to begin. For those who have already begun the journey, let not the war make them turn back in fear. Christ is the guide and companion on this journey of the soul to God. Without Christ we would be desperately alone and would not even enter the gates of the castle. To enter, one must pray. If one falls in prayer, there is only one way to rise: pray again.

J.P. Can you briefly describe this castle and the dwelling place within? As a metaphor, your castle image is both elaborate yet quite simple.

MOTHER I cannot describe every room of the castle for there are many above and below, but I shall walk with you through the seven mansions. Now, it was in a vision that God showed me how the human soul is a beautiful castle of very clear diamond or crystal which, as I said, has many rooms, perhaps not unlike the cabin of the Thomas Merton fellow you mentioned earlier. Now this may sound foolish to say that your soul is a castle, because if it is, you don't have to enter it since it is already within you. That would be like telling someone to go into a room that he or she is already in. This, however, is exactly what I am saying for there are many ways of being inside yourself. There are some people, for example, who have no idea whatsoever that God awaits them within with perfect love. It is God himself who resides in the central mansion of the soul, awaiting your arrival. If you begin with courage and determination, committing yourself to the journey, the King will call. Everyone is invited to rest in union yet so few take up the journey.

J.P. As you describe this castle and king, I can think only of the opening line of the Our Father.

MOTHER Yes, the rooms of the castle are like the many dwelling places in heaven.

J.P. So, through prayer and recollection, one can begin the journey inward to the King, responding to the King's call. We have begun the journey with prayer. What then?

MOTHER Yes. We have opened the gate of the castle by prayer, by spending some time each day simply talking with God in solitary conversation. One should not feel unworthy to pray or become trapped by false humility. The worst illness that ever attacked me was when I decided to abandon prayer because I thought myself too sinful. Souls without prayer are like a person whose legs or arms are paralyzed, so concerned perhaps with worldly affairs, riches, and wealth, that their souls become numb. Such people are unable to open the gates of the castle except through prayer. When opening the doors of the castle, however, all sorts of insects and vermin can slip in with you. These are the preoccupations we all have with the outside world, with reputation, appearance, possessions, business and other seemingly important matters. There is very little of the King's heat and light reaching these outer rooms of the mansion, so one must work hard to detach from all these preoccupations in order to gather together and recollect for the journey. Actually, the first part of the journey into the castle requires primarily your own effort and work. It is you who must respond to the call, pray, and open the gate. Let go of the beasts that bother, the insects that pick, and pray, pray, and pray.

As you travel through the first three mansions (not, of course, traveling in some orderly fashion, one after the other, but perhaps going into yourself and then running out again in fear), you have to build your own aqueducts to carry the waters that will help. It is very important to listen to good sermons, read devotional books, join in with good friends, talk with others on the journey. All of this can help you in the battle against the voices of evil that tell you to go no further. The devil will remind you constantly how much you have and must give up if you take this journey, not telling you what will be gained if you do; peace in God. I often recommend as people do battle with the evil voice that speaks against the journey, that they remember and look upon the cross of Christ who gave all for all to be love in all. As we look on the cross in recollection, patience may arise to help us on our journey, patience with ourselves. We must not expect to make the full journey overnight or to think we do it on our own. As we progress from room to room we come to recognize how truly little we can do for ourselves and how much we depend upon the strength and love of the King. With all the virtuous work in the world, we cannot force our way into the center of ourselves, into the castle of the King. The closer we come to God, the more we recognize even virtuous accomplishments must be let go of. The only way to proceed through the third mansion is to do so with great humility.

J.P. I knew you would be getting to the subject of humility. It is a concept and attitude that is much misunderstood in my time.

MOTHER As in mine as well. As I mentioned earlier, perhaps it is because so many exaggerate their unworthiness. Truth is the foundation of the castle. Walking hand in hand with truth is humility. It is God who is everlasting truth. To be humble is to know that of ourselves we have nothing good, but nothingness and emptiness. If you don't understand this, you live a lie. The more you see yourself in the light of supreme truth the more you please God and journey on to the king.

J.P. So from our perspective in comparison to the Creator, creation is nothing; but from the Creator's perspective, creatureliness is everything.

MOTHER Yes, well put. Once you know this truth, you can live more freely. You can allow God to carry you deeper and deeper into the castle that is you. In humility you learn not to look upon yourself as better than others or even to be concerned of what others may think of you. In humble truth you learn that you are a slave with God as master. Understanding such, you conform your will to God.

J.P. You mentioned how we can easily exaggerate this perspective into a false sense of humility. There are many in my time who have misunderstood the truth of humility. They get stuck in a self-depreciating illness that refuses to recognize the beauty of God's creation. They negate, negate, negate without allowing God to bless, bless, bless. Some of this misunderstanding comes from a distortion of the writings of your wise companion, John of the Cross. I believe I understand when you say we must see ourselves as a slave of God, servant, nothing of ourselves. For example, to realistically assess, a humble person must be ready to accept legitimate criticism, their faith placed before God and others and to deal with the narcissistic tendencies and illusions of grandiosity, lack of care for other's needs, inappropriate need for attention, and the striving for personal perfection. A humble person is not narcissistic in self-esteem but rather recognizes their value as one of God's esteemed.

MOTHER With such an attitude, one can move through the third room into the fourth where it is God who now begins to flow freely, gathering all into harmony. Here one notices a general sense of drawing inward. The outer world is losing its hold as you begin to experience in the quiet of God what you once lost. Here our prayer changes from an active recollection to a more passive prayer where even the mind becomes still. The soul of a person here may experience deep but fleeting experiences when it realizes how close God is. Here the King sees the intense desire of people of good will and draws them closer to his mercy. Here we experience such a longing for solitude that we gradually sink into ourselves like a turtle or hedgehog. No longer do we have to work to fill the water trough for a drink of peace, for God now fills the trough from the very source. The spring of God's love flows freely now. Mind and memory, passions and will, are gathered together by God's quiet voice. As you progress ever closer to the center of the castle, the King speaks more and more softly until there is no sound at all, only harmony. When you enter the sixth mansion of the castle, God reveals in visions and raptures that surprise and delight you, while making you also more humble, silent, anxious for solitude, and able to bear tremendous burdens for the Lord's work.

J.P. Visions and raptures abound among some in my time as well. We have Christians of all sorts claiming to hear God's voice, some in prayer towers, others in private revelations which at times stand in opposition to the community's faith. I personally wonder if the manifestation of visions and raptures is not frequently the individual's unconscious need to feel important or special.

MOTHER I have cautioned many about paying excessive attention to raptures as though they prove one's holiness. Let me only say that true revealing raptures are not of your own making, but are for God's purpose only. Let us return to our journey to the center of the castle, however. Thus far, Father John, we have journeyed from the first rooms marked by the prayer of recollection into the prayer of quiet and on into the prayer of deeper and deeper union. In the sixth and seventh rooms of the castle the door between the rooms remains open so that God can reveal in the last room what I cannot explain, not having reached it. In the center mansion, though, the marriage between soul and King takes place. The soul is no longer blind to God's ways. What works you do now in service of God are marked by love rather than greatness. Here the hot blade of the soul plunged into cold water cools so that steel and water are balanced in temperature. Calm and quiet are the signs of such a spouse, no matter the work or sufferings that must be carried. I make no claim to be in such union with the King.

J.P. The images of your story of the journey weave in and out almost falling upon one another. May I share a story of a young man and king that for me captures some of what you have said, in far less detail of course.

MOTHER Surely, Father. I am weary of talking anyway.

J.P. "There was a householder's son who went away into a distant country. During the boy's absence, the father accumulated immeasurable riches while the son became miserably poor. The son, while searching for food and clothing, happened to come to the country in which his father lived. One day the father saw his son in his wretched condition, ragged and brutalized by poverty, and was so moved that he ordered some of his servants to call the boy to his home.

"When the son saw the house to which he was conducted by the servants, he thought that he must have evoked the suspicion of a powerful man, and that he would be thrown into prison. Full of apprehension, he made his escape from the rich man's house before he had seen his father.

"The father again sent servants out after his son, who

caught and brought him back in spite of his cries and lamentations. When the boy was returned home again, the father ordered his servants to deal tenderly with him. The father then appointed a laborer of his son's rank and education to employ the lad as a helpmate on the estate. The son was very pleased with his new situation.

"Every day from the window of the palace the father watched the boy and when he saw that he was honest and industrious, he promoted him in rank higher and higher.

"After some time, the father summoned his son and all the servants together to tell them the secret that the boy was truly his child. The poor boy was shocked, yet full of joy at meeting his father."

The story ends, Mother, with this significant line: "Little by little must human minds be trained for higher truths."

MOTHER A tender story, Father, and so true. Did not Jesus take on our rank to labor for our salvation? It is Jesus who prepares us to meet the king. Did not the poor boy learn what we all must? That God the Father and King makes, saves, endures, calls, and awaits us no matter how far we stray. Like the boy in the story, we are all worried what God will ask of us. Will he give us life or death, sickness or health, shame or honor, war or swelling peace, weakness or full strength? To all of life we must say our yes, to wisdom or ignorance, abundant years or famine and hunger, darkness or sunlight, being moved here or there. Life can indeed be troublesome and painful, yet like the boy of your story we too can discover our Father's love. We, too, can say to God in joy and gladness, "Yours I am, for from you I was born. What is it you want me to do?"

J.P. What comes to mind as you say that, Mother, is Jesus in the garden who turns his will to the Father and submits to love. (At this point in our conversation, a flurry of noise arose from behind Mother Teresa and Sister Maria. Two other sisters entered the parlor quickly, whispering to each other and then to Sister Maria and Mother Teresa. After only a moment or two, Mother spoke.)

MOTHER I'm sorry, Father, but we must end our visit. There is rumor about our beloved Fray John. They speak of his being tortured. I must consider what actions can be taken. I have already written the King and Superior General. I can't think of much else to do. However, the sisters are greatly upset, so we are going to the chapel to pray for his safety. A conversation with the laboring Christ of your story would be of help now. We need a helpmate in our cause.

J.P. I would not hold you from such prayer. Thank you for your time, Mother.

MOTHER Now wait, Father. You know how we battle to be established as a separate community of Discalced religious and you know that our faithful Fray John suffers kidnapping and torture, but you also are from the future. How do these urgent problems go for us?

J.P. Well, Mother, I'm not sure if I should....

MOTHER I know, Father, that I should not ask you but rather should depend on the will of the Father. But as my sisters know, I am at times inconsistent and difficult to live with. God must do his work and I the work given. Tell me how does it go. I pray it will go well.

J.P. Let me say, Mother, only that you will win your battles, both outer and inner.

Mother Teresa of Jesus died in the city of Alba, Oct. 4, 1582, at the age of 77. As a shrewd, pragmatic, self-possessed woman who combined mystic genius with a subtle sense of civil ecclesiastical politics, Teresa was able to win the battle to establish a separate reformed order of Discalced Carmelites. On June 22, 1580, papal approval was given and on March 3, 1581, the separation was formally in effect, with Rev. Jerome Gracian elected first provincial. Fray John of the Cross on August 17, 1578, escaped from the Carmelite jail in Toledo by his own devices and spent the remainder of his life assisting Mother Teresa and writing books, including his most famous *Ascent of Mount Carmel*. Mother Teresa continued to found convents, work for reform, and write. Her works included not only her *Life, The Way of Perfection, The Interior Castle, Conceptions on the Love of God, The Book of the Foundations,* but hundreds of letters as well as a bit of poetry. Teresa was canonized a saint in 1622 and declared a Doctor of the church by Pope Paul VI in 1967.

Suggested Readings

Teresa of Avila: The Interior Castle, transl. Kieran Kavanaugh, O.C.D. and Otilio Rodriguez, O.C.D. (The Classics of Western Spirituality). Mahwah, N.J.: Paulist Press, 1979.

St. Teresa of Avila: The Collected Works, vols. I, II, trans. Kieran Kavanaugh, O.C.D. and Otilio Rodriguez, O.C.D. Washington, D.C.: Institute of Carmelite Studies, 1976.

Teresa of Avila, by Marcelle Auclair. Garden City, N.Y.: Doubleday, 1959.

Teresa: A Woman, by Victoria Lincoln.. Albany: State Univ. of N.Y. Press, 1984.

Christian Mysticism: The Future of a Tradition, by Harvey D. Egan, S.J. New York: Pueblo Publ. Co., 1984.

Spiritual Pilgrims: Carl Jung & Teresa of Avila, by John Welch, O. Carm. Mahwah, N.J.: Paulist Press, 1982.

Meditations with Teresa of Avila, A Centering Book, by Camille Campbell. Santa Fe, N.M.: Bear & Co., 1985.

Teresa de Jesus: A Secular Appreciation by Walker Lowry. One hundred twenty-five copies of this book printed for Walker Lowry at Stinehour Press, 1977.

The Doctrine of Teresa de Jesus by Walker Lowry. One hundred copies of this book printed for Walker Lowry at the Stinehour Press, 1984.

Excerpts
from the writings of
TERESA OF AVILA

"Today while beseeching our Lord to speak for me because I wasn't able to think of anything to say, nor did I know how to begin to carry out this obedience, there came to mind what I shall now speak about, that which will provide us with a basis to begin with. It is that we consider our soul to be like a castle made entirely out of a diamond or of very clear crystal, in which there are many rooms, just as in heaven there are many dwelling places."

Interior Castles

"Well, getting back to our beautiful and delightful castle we must see how we can enter it. It seems I'm saying something foolish. For if this castle is the soul, clearly one doesn't have to enter it since it is within oneself. How foolish it would seem were we to tell someone to enter a room he is already in. But you must understand that there is a great difference in the ways one may be inside the castle. For there are many souls who are in the outer courtyard—which is where the guards stay—and don't care at all about entering the castle, nor do they know what lies within that most precious place, nor who is within, nor even how many rooms it has. You have already heard in some books on prayer that the soul is advised to enter within itself; well that's the very thing I'm advising. Insofar as I can understand, the gate of entry to this castle is prayer and reflection."

Interior Castles

"For never, however exalted the soul may be, is anything else more fitting than self-knowledge; nor could it be even were the soul to so desire."

Interior Castles

"This is the reason for prayer, my daughters, the purpose of this spiritual marriage: the birth always of good works, good works."

Interior Castles

"Believe me. In the presence of Infinite wisdom, one act of humility is worth more than all the knowledge of the world."

The Book of Her Life

"And since he doesn't force our will, He takes what we give Him; but He doesn't give Himself completely until we give ourselves completely."

The Way of Perfection

"...we shouldn't build castles in the air. The Lord doesn't look so much at the greatness of our works as at the love with which they are done."

Interior Castles

"You will be immediately told that speaking with...[a friend] is unnecessary, that it is enough to have God. But a good means to having God is to speak with His friends."

The Way of Perfection

"Some books on prayer tell us where one must seek God. Within oneself, very clearly, is the best place to look...."

The Book of Her Life

CONCLUSION

From the massive amount of research necessary to actually write these seven interviews, and from the actual imaginative interviews I conducted through this research, I have learned much about Christian spirituality as well as about myself.

From the experience of interviewing hundreds of men and women on radio and television, I can testify that seldom do you finish an interview without the feeling that you were just getting started. If the interviewer has a strong curiosity and the guest comes to life, both should walk away from an interview with more questions and insights than time allowed, often thinking back on what was said and how it could have been said better or more clearly. These interviews only scratch the surface of these mystics' messages and lives.

Despite the brevity of the interviews, I have learned the secret of the mystics. A story may help in the telling. When I was 15 years old, I was employed, through a coincidence full of God, at a monastery-retreat house near my home, to wash dishes and wait on tables for the guests on retreat. On weekends I would do this work under the strong guidance of a few brothers, while catching glimpses of the many more priests and brothers in the monastery proper or walking outside.

I am not sure if many of the other wide-eyed teens with

whom I worked ever thought of joining the monastery, but I did, primarily, I thought then, to know the secret. My youthful, overactive imagination told me that when young brothers took vows, as they called it, they were told the one secret for a happy life, that some old and venerable teacher would tell it to them once and life would be forever changed and peaceful.

Years later, to the surprise of some, I took those same vows, fantasizing perhaps, hoping perchance, that the secret would also be told to me. I was right. I, too, learned the secret of the mystics, the secret of peaceful living.

It did not take place as I had dreamed, with a kindly old father whispering in my ears a one-sentence answer. Although I have been greatly blessed to have deeply generous spiritual guides, no one handed me the secret of the mystics on a plastic platter. No, it was living itself and the gentle trying to turn again and again, getting up, falling down, standing up, crashing down, moving closer, and running in evasion that has taught me the secret of life—a life with God. The big secret is that there is no secret.

Experiencing God and living with divine aliveness every day is not for the select few who have gnostic knowledge or ecclesiastical vows. In fact, a dominant intellect, overwhelming emotions, or a rigid structure can at times be a hindrance to the mystery that God is. The secret is God, the Numinous, Jesus, the Power of Mystery is available to all in all for the good of all.

Learning such a secret, however, does not grant one easy access to pleasurable living, for with the ever-present God comes even greater responsibility. A mystic knows the only power that can change anything from human hearts to cultural hostility is the love of the creator for the created.

Just as there is no secret that another can tell you that will lift the responsibility for your spiritual journey off what may already be sagging shoulders, so there can be no honest walking toward God alone. Identity may be found in solitude, but it is lived out in the company of community, for the betterment of evolving consciousness and justice.

What the mensches taught me in these interviews, or reminded me of once again, is that as God is for all so we must be.

Dom Raphael Simon, a Trappist monk and psychiatrist, tells us in his extraordinary book, *Hammer and Fire,* what ultimately happens when you open yourself to the affirming presence of God in life: "a transformation of the human personality. When enough people have realized this transformation, society itself will be transformed... If the spiritual life is pursued prudently, in accord with sound advice, it increases the psychological resources of people, and their mental health as well as human development." [14]

I am generally not a prophet of doom, yet I must agree with Rayner Torkington who writes in *Peter Calvay: Prophet,* a spiritual fiction filled with the message that the only thing that can radically change society and each of us is religion. It is not politics or psychotherapy, although both can be used as healing tools.

> Politics is only the art of the possible—religion is the art of the impossible. Only religion, or a relationship of love with God, can change human hearts from the inside. This is why I [and those interviewed in this book] keep emphasizing prayer, not because prayer changes God's heart, but because it changes the human heart. Only in this way will humanity be changed from the inside, so that they can live safely and in peace on the outside with fellow humans, whom they are called to love and live with as brother and sister. [15]

Each mystic in this book and the mystics among us are balanced human beings who, as Torkington describes, "are not so lost in a self-indugent evangelical piosity that he or she forgets the physical needs of others, nor so engrossed in a sociopolitical involvement that he forgets the spiritual needs of himself."[16]

A mystic is ultimately resilient in mind, heart, and

prayer, ready to bend when grace nudges in a certain direction. The mystics are always ready to gently turn in the direction of divinity, as a ballet dancer so graciously turns to her partner for arms that will embrace for the next movement.

When I was doing research for this book, I read a number of books that described the personality of the mystic. Among the many books, one stands out as helpful in presenting the characteristics of a person who is mentally stable yet open to creative intuition: *Resilience* by Frederic Flach, M.D.

Dr. Flach describes resiliency as "the psychological and biological [I would add "spiritual"] strengths required to successfully master change."[17] Once you add the spiritual element of gifted grace to this definition of resiliency, you have an excellent word to describe the mystics of the medieval period that I interviewed and the mystics who will survive and grow in the struggles of today and the future. Times may change and so outer circumstances, but yet the human capacity to deal with living remains somewhat constant. So too does the love of God.

In the light of the mystics of yesterday, today, and tomorrow, I read Dr. Flach's list of attributes of the resilient personality. They describe well the persons of Hildegard, Mechtild, Eckhart, Van Ruysbroeck, Tauler, Julian, and Teresa for each shares to a remarkable degree:

- A strong, supple sense of self-esteem.
- Independence of thought and action, without fear of relying on others or reluctance to do so.
- The ability to give and take in one's interactions with others, and a well established network of personal friends, including one or more who serve as confidants.
- A high level of personal discipline and a sense of responsibility.
- Recognition and development of one's special gifts and talents.
- Open-mindedness and receptivity to new ideas.

- A willingness to dream.
- A wide range of interests.
- A keen sense of humor.
- Insight into one's own feelings and those of others, and the ability to communicate these in an appropriate manner.
- A high tolerance of distress.
- Focus, a commitment to life, and a philosophical framework within which personal experiences can be interpreted with meaning and hope, even at life's seemingly most hopeless moments.[18]

Resilient as each of the mystics I have interviewed were so also did they struggle, like all others in life. Mystics are not exempt from the neurotic battles of mind and body that are part of the process of growth and transformation, nor are they entitled to a claim on infallible decisions. The mystics in this book were not perfect, as though without flaw, but they were rather perfect in the sense that they gave everything to God, their sinfulness, psychological troubles, and physical ailments, as well as their successes, joys, failures, and talents.

In the final analysis, what lives most fully through the lives of those closest to God is soul. Mystics are never so much self-actualized (in the ego sense) as they are soul-actualized. In so being, they become exceptionally healthy and holy people.

From all that I have learned from these mystics, and shared herein, perhaps the most important lesson is how much each loved and cherished the religious tradition to which he or she belonged. All were faithful to their Christian heritage, even if they were at times moved to criticize church bureaucracy. They were dedicated first to climb the mystic mountain in their own backyards.

There is no doubt that Hildegard, Mechtild, Eckhart, Jan Van Ruysbroeck, John Tauler, Julian, and Teresa had experiences of God that were creatively orthodox. They were daring people, imaginative in metaphor, and artistically inventive in their God description, yet humble in the truth of their own inconsistency. They were resilient people, forever ready to hear God where God spoke, even if it challenged the very structure of faith they accepted so well. They were the holy human men and women of yesterday who have shown us how to climb the mountain of God that rises before us, with eyes that see in the dark.

Suggested Readings in Mysticism

Mysticism, by Evelyn Underhill. New York: New American Library, 1955.

Understanding Mysticism, ed. Richard Woods, O.P. Garden City, N.Y.: Doubleday, 1980.

The Study of Spirituality, ed. Cheslyn Jones, Geoffrey Wainwright, Edward Yarnold, S.J. New York: Oxford University Press, 1986.

Fire & Light: The Saints & Theology, by William M. Thompson. Mahwah, N.J.: Paulist Press, 1987.

Discovering God Within, by John R. Yungblut. Philadelphia: Westminster Press, 1979.

What Are They Saying About Mysticism, by Harvey D. Egan, S.J. Mahwah, N.J.: Paulist Press, 1982.

Light From Light: An Anthology of Christian Mysticism, ed. Louis Dupre and James A. Wiseman, O.S.B. Mahwah, N.J.: Paulist Press,1988.

Notes

Introductory Letter

1. Mary Wolf-Salin, *No Other Light* (New York: Crossroad 1987), p. 19.
2. Harold Kushner, *When All You've Wanted Isn't Enough* (New York: Simon and Schuster, 1986), p. 134-135.

Hildegard of Bingen

3. Joseph Campbell, *The Power of Myth* (Garden City, N.Y.: Doubleday Inc., 1988), p. 34.
4. Jean Hardy, *A Psychology with a Soul: Psychosynthesis in Evolutionary Context* (London and New York: Routledge and Kegan Paul, 1987), p. 110.

Meister Eckhart

5. Walter Burghardt, S.J., *Tell The Next Generation: Homilies and Near Homilies* (New York: Paulist Press, 1980), p. 138.

Johannes Tauler

6. Karl Rahner, *Theological Investigations VII* (New York: Herder and Herder, 1971), p. 12.
7. William James, *Principles of Psychology* vol. I (New York: Dover Publications, 1950), p. 127.
8. William Bausch, *Take Heart, Father* (Mystic, Conn.: Twenty-Third Publications, 1986), p. 195.

Julian of Norwich

9. *Prayers and Meditations of St. Anselm,* translated by Sr. Benedicta Ward (Middlesex, England: Penguin Books, 1973), p. 155.
10. Thomas Merton, *Seeds of Destruction* (New York: Farrar, Straus and Giroux, 1961), p. 275.

Teresa of Avila

11. Thomas Merton, *Raids on the Unspeakable* (New York: New Direction Publications, 1966), p. 10.
12. Maggie Ross, *The Fire and the Furnace* (Mahwah, N.J.: Paulist Press, 1987), p. 23.
13. *Just Open a Vein,* ed. William Brohaugh (Cincinnati: Writers Digest Books, 1987), p. 84.

Conclusion

14. Dom Raphael Simon, O.S.C.O., M.D., *Hammer and Fire* (Petersham, Mass: St. Bedes Publications, 1987), p. xviii.
15. Rayner Torkington, *Peter Calvay: Prophet* (Liverpool: Spennithorne Publications, 1987), p. 175.
16. Torkington, p. 155.
17. Dr. Frederic Flach, M.D., *Resilience; Discovering a New Strength at Times of Stress* (New York: Ballantine Books, 1988), p. xi.
18. Flach, p. 114.

What the critics say about John Powers's *Mirror, Mirror on the Wall: The Art of Talking with Yourself* and *If They Could Speak: Ten Witnesses to the Passion of Jesus...*

"*Mirror, Mirror on the Wall,* so sensitive to human pain, offers an invitation to enter [God's] kingdom, to give names, as Adam did, to the animals within us, and to begin to know ourselves even as we are known and loved by God."

Eugene Kennedy
Author of *The Joy of Being Human*

"In *Mirror, Mirror on the Wall,* Father Powers convinces us that it is important for people to explore their 'inner family' and deal with all their conflicting emotions, habits, and feelings.

Peggy Weber
The Catholic Observer

"We always want to eavesdrop upon the secret conversations of the saints. And there is something mischievous about each of us that makes us want to sidle up to those less than saintly persons in the Bible and find out what they are thinking, or to the saints in their less than saintly moments. In *If They Could Speak* Fr. Powers allows us to satisfy these hopes, conversing with the *sleeping* disciple James, the *despairing* Judas, the *mocking* soldier, along with Mary the *Mother* and John the *Beloved.* We walk away from this book seeing the saints more human than we thought and the sinners more saintly than we ever gave them credit for."

Carroll Stuhmueller, CP
Catholic Theological Union

"What were the thoughts of those directly involved in the cruel and swift crucifixion of Jesus? In *If They Could Speak* Father Powers uses his considerable imaginative skill to reflect on ten witnesses of Christ's passion. Each speaks to his or her (and our own) share in the most pivotal event in Christian History. They give a sense of 'being there.'"

Spiritual Book News

Mirror, Mirror on the Wall: The Art of Talking with Yourself, and *If They Could Speak: Ten Witnesses to the Passion of Jesus* by John Powers, are available through religious bookstores or Twenty-Third Publications, 185 Willow Street, Mystic, CT, 1-800-321-0411.

POWERS, REV. JOHN D., O.P.

Holy & Human Mystics for Our Times